CANADA IS *NOT* BACK

HOW JUSTIN TRUDEAU IS IN OVER HIS HEAD ON FOREIGN POLICY

JOCELYN COULON
TRANSLATED BY GEORGE TOMBS

JAMES LORIMER & COMPANY LTD., PUBLISHERS
TORONTO

Originally published in French as *Un selfie avec Justin Trudeau* by Québec Amérique.

Translated into English by George Tombs.

Published in Canada in 2019.

James Lorimer & Company Ltd., Publishers acknowledges funding support from the Ontario Arts Council (OAC), an agency of the Government of Ontario. We acknowledge the support of the Canada Council for the Arts, which last year invested $153 million to bring the arts to Canadians throughout the country. This project has been made possible in part by the Government of Canada and with the support of Ontario Creates.

Cover design: Tyler Cleroux
Cover image: THE CANADIAN PRESS/Sean Kilpatrick

Library and Archives Canada Cataloguing in Publication

Title: Canada is not back : how Justin Trudeau is in over his head on foreign policy / Jocelyn Coulon; George Tombs, translator.

Other titles: Selfie avec Justin Trudeau. English

Names: Coulon, Jocelyn. | Tombs, George, translator.

Description: Translation of: Un selfie avec Justin Trudeau : regard critique sur la diplomatie du premier ministre. | Includes bibliographical references and index.

Identifiers: Canadiana (print) 20190063823 | Canadiana (ebook) 20190063874 | ISBN 9781459413344 (softcover) | ISBN 9781459413351 (EPUB)

Subjects: LCSH: Trudeau, Justin. | LCSH: Canada—Foreign relations—21st century. | LCSH: Diplomacy. | CSH: Canada—Politics and government—2015-

Classification: LCC FC655 .C6813 2019 | DDC 971.07/4—dc23

James Lorimer & Company Ltd., Publishers
117 Peter Street, Suite 304
Toronto, ON, Canada
M5V 0M3
www.lorimer.ca

Printed and bound in Canada.

CONTENTS

To Elaine Potvin, friend and colleague

FOREWORD

Modern life tends to spare us intellectual and physical effort. In the place of imagination, it feeds us with images . . . It provides us with every convenience, every means of reaching our objectives easily, without the struggle of actually getting there.

— Paul Valéry, French poet and philosopher

This book deals with a man, Justin Trudeau, and with his idea of Canada's place on the international scene. He was famous even before becoming prime minister. His name had broad appeal, in Canada and abroad. His stunning electoral victory in October 2015 sent shock waves around the world, raising hopes for his leadership and for the country he was about to lead.

During the election campaign, Trudeau promised to recover Canada's place in international affairs. This would mean breaking with a decade of Conservative policies that, for many, had isolated the country, plunging it into the dark ages. During the campaign, the Liberals summed up their foreign policy agenda with a single catchy slogan: "Canada is back." Trudeau set the bar high, and for good reason. Since the end of the Second World War, Canada had enjoyed an enviable reputation around the world. Canadian leaders and diplomats had contributed significantly to the creation of the international system as we know it today. Canada was one of the founders of the United Nations and NATO and had made significant investments in these institutions. Among the many original Canadian contributions to the world order, the creation of the UN peacekeepers — the Blue Helmets — is the best known. Canada had not only been a factor of peace in the world, but had been ready to use force when the international situation required it.

During their decade in power, the Conservatives had refocused this international role, promoting the use of force instead. The Blue Helmets had been replaced by steel helmets. Opinion polls had consistently shown that Canadians were uncomfortable with this new role for the country.

Trudeau understood the gap between Conservative government policy and public expectations. He sought to restore the balance, providing voters with an ambitious election platform that skillfully combined tradition and innovation. Trudeau's platform offered voters the prospect of Canada re-engaging with the United Nations, taking part once again in UN peacekeeping missions, and deepening economic and military ties with the United States. The platform marked a departure from Conservative policies in other ways: for example, in the welcoming of refugees and migrants, the fight against climate change, the war against terrorism, the increase in foreign aid to developing countries, the protection of women and girls in conflict zones, and the diversification of the Canadian economy by opening up to developing markets.

It is now time for an honest assessment. Undeniably, Trudeau's arrival in office was well received practically everywhere in the world. Wherever he has gone, he has left an impression of dynamism, openness and listening. His rhetoric about diversity, tolerance and generosity has come as a breath of fresh air at a time when hate speech and xenophobia are undermining societies and fostering the emergence of populist voices. He has called for multilateralism and free trade, where others have trumpeted isolationism and protectionism. Still, it is worth asking whether Trudeau walks the talk — whether his actions as prime minister correspond to his compelling words. What has become of the ambitious goal of restoring Canada's role on the world scene?

If the Trudeau government's concrete actions are compared with its public statements, it is clear that the promise of bringing Canada back has not been fulfilled. In practice, the Liberal foreign policy agenda does not represent a break with Conservative policies, but a continuation. Moreover, the prime minister cannot take credit for a single international initiative. "Canada is back" seems to be pretty much an empty slogan.

How has this happened? Is this negative assessment justified?

These are the questions I seek to answer in this book. I bear some responsibility for what happened in Ottawa after the Liberal victory in 2015. I played a part in developing the prime minister's foreign policy. I witnessed how it was developed and implemented. I was a member of the foreign policy advisory council Trudeau created before the 2015 election campaign: between May 2014 and May 2015, the council met with him often. As part of the council, I helped articulate the Liberal Party's policy stances on peacekeeping, Africa, multilateralism and military interventions. Once the Liberals took office, I was named political adviser to Stéphane Dion, the minister of foreign affairs. I held that position for a year, from February 2016 to late January 2017, when Dion was replaced by Chrystia Freeland. I worked with Dion on many of the above files.

As a result, this book provides an insider's perspective. I explain and describe the continuity of analyses and decisions, as well as the reasoning, if any, behind them. I have based this book on the discussions we had on the advisory council, my notes taken from day to day, documents and speeches, conversations I had after my departure and my knowledge of the history of Canadian foreign policy. My eyewitness account follows the trajectory of the Trudeau government's foreign policy as closely as possible. I don't claim to provide a comprehensive view; the account you will find in these pages is necessarily partial — I deal with high-profile issues or the ones I know best.

In the first part of this book, I follow Justin Trudeau's intellectual development before he went into politics. I describe the relationship he had with his father, the ambiguous choices he made in terms of education and intellectual effort, the lessons he drew from his travels abroad, and the professional and political paths he pursued. This part of the book reveals a man who is unconcerned with world affairs, who demonstrated little or no real interest in foreign policy before becoming leader of the Liberal Party.

The next two parts of the book cover the exercise of power following the 2015 election, highlighting the files I dealt with during my year in Stéphane Dion's office. I describe Justin Trudeau as a man who gained power without international experience or any clear concept of his foreign policy. He took active and decisive positions on China and the reception of refugees and migrants, but wavering and ambivalent stances on most other issues. He yielded to pressure groups, whereas he ought to uphold the national interest by developing a long-term strategic vision. He is influenced more by opinion polls and the media than by the advice of his ambassadors and diplomats. Finally, I show Trudeau's inability to establish a working relationship with Dion, ultimately firing him without a valid reason.

Trudeau has a particular conception of power. As he has written in his memoirs, *Common Ground*, he loves direct, first-hand contact with people, which helps him understand their desires and aspirations. While reaching out to others, however, he doesn't spend enough time studying his files and getting to the bottom of things. He reigns more than he governs.

He also loves cultivating a self-image on the world scene,

relying on selfies and interviews with trendy magazines like *Paris Match* or *Vogue*. Image-making, he says, is an essential part of governing.[1]

The prime minister is not wrong in ascribing such importance to communication. But there comes a point where ideas need to be distinguished clearly from compelling images. A political leader captivated by image-making risks losing touch with the ideas that need to drive foreign and domestic policy.

Jocelyn Coulon
February 2019

PART 1

JUSTIN TRUDEAU'S INTELLECTUAL JOURNEY

CHAPTER ONE

CHAPTER ONE

THE BIRTH OF A POLITICIAN

Foreign policy was front and centre during the 2015 election campaign. In fact, the leaders of the three main parties — Justin Trudeau for the Liberals, Stephen Harper for the Conservatives and Thomas Mulcair for the New Democrats — agreed to take part in a TV debate devoted to foreign policy. This was the first-ever televised leaders' debate on foreign policy during a Canadian election campaign. Foreign policy had been a factor during the 1988 campaign, but mainly as part of the economic aspect, due to the heated debate around the North American Free Trade Agreement (NAFTA).

Since 2000, a worrisome series of crises and phenomena — from climate change to Islamist terrorism and the emergence of new powers on the world scene — affected the international order, in place since 1945. This raised serious questions that few men and women in political life were in a position to address, let alone solve. The new world order was too fluid, too erratic. Even so, it was vitally important to discuss world affairs, to reflect on the nature and pace of change, and to understand public anxieties in Canada — a country no longer sheltered from the clamour of world events.

On October 20 and 22, 2014, almost a year to the day before the TV debate, two Canadian terrorists — both professed

Islamists — had murdered members of the Armed Forces in Saint-Jean-sur-Richelieu and Ottawa. The terrorist in Ottawa managed to enter the federal Parliament, where he tried to kill employees and elected representatives. These attacks proved deeply shocking for the public at large as well as for the political community.

This was the setting for the televised debate on foreign policy on September 28, 2015, at the Munk School of Global Affairs and Public Policy at the University of Toronto. The three leaders crossed swords for two hours, answering ten questions before an often highly partisan audience. The discussion was lively and sometimes confused, as is to be expected when several political leaders engage in public debate. At the time, gauging who won and who lost the debate really depended on one's political affiliation. Justin Trudeau came off rather well. But nothing in his performance was left to chance. Nothing in his education or election as Liberal Party leader in 2013 indicated he took the slightest interest in world affairs; his foreign policy advisers coached him extensively, helping him prepare for specific policy questions. I will come back to this point in more detail in the next chapter.

***

Justin Trudeau was not the son of an ordinary father. Pierre Elliott Trudeau was a lawyer by training, a liberal intellectual, one of the founders of the journal *Cité libre*; he was also a playboy and bon vivant. He managed not to get conscripted into the Army during the Second World War, then travelled around the world after the war ended. He whihihent to China, touring the country by bicycle. In 1960, he headed back to China a second time along with his friend Jacques Hébert, who was later named senator. The two men wrote a memorable book about their experience, *Two Innocents in Red China*.[1]

Trudeau entered federal politics upon returning to Canada. In 1967, he was appointed minister of justice in the government of Lester B. Pearson. Trudeau was a formidable public speaker, thanks to a combination of intelligence, a capacity for forthright repartee and eloquence. He dominated debates, and his adversaries came to dread him. Trudeau arrived on the Canadian scene at a particular moment in time. The winds of change and protest were blowing across the Western world. He understood this desire for change, and as justice minister introduced ground-breaking measures, amending the Criminal Code to legalize abortion and homosexuality. On a personal level, he created his own style, dressing and behaving just as he pleased. He sported elegant clothes and a rose in his buttonhole, dated movie stars and disregarded official protocol. This period saw the birth of Trudeaumania. Just one year after entering the federal Cabinet, he was voted party leader and became prime minister. He called an election and won a crushing majority in June 1968. At the beginning of 1971, he married Margaret Sinclair, with whom he had three sons: Justin, Alexandre and Michel.

By the time Pierre Trudeau came to power, he had a good understanding of foreign affairs. This interest in the world was greatly stimulated by his travels as a young man. Besides co-authoring a book on China, he wrote articles in *Cité libre*, starting in 1951, about the Korean War, Canada's economic dependency on the United States and the nature of war. In 1963, in a final article on foreign policy, he took Pearson to task for allowing the United States to station nuclear weapons on Canadian soil,[2] even refusing to become a Liberal candidate for this reason. Trudeau patched things up with the Liberals two years later, however, and was elected to the House of Commons in 1965.

As soon as he became prime minister, Trudeau wanted a complete reboot of Canadian foreign and defence policy, breaking free from the ideological stranglehold of the Cold War.[3] The world had changed since the end of the Second World War and the beginning of Cold War in 1948. Trudeau realized that the world had become multipolar. The North–South divide posed a greater threat than the rivalry between East and West, which in any case was subsiding thanks to the policy of détente.

Trudeau wanted his government to get back to basics and rethink everything, including Canada's membership in NATO. He even considered the idea of Canada becoming a neutral country. He believed Canada's foreign and defence policy had for too long been dictated by outside forces, by commitments that were incompatible with Canada's own security or direct interests. He dreamed of developing a foreign policy that would serve Canada's national interests. Revamping foreign and defence policy also meant addressing Canada's economic dependency on the United States, which had a huge impact on the choices Ottawa made. As a way of reducing this dependency, Trudeau strove to diversify the country's trade, reaching out to Asia, Europe and Latin America, and strengthening Canadian control of sectors of the economy that were largely in foreign hands.[4]

This policy reboot led to the publication of a policy guidance document about Canadian diplomacy and the white paper on defence. The first of these documents, *Foreign Policy for Canadians*, recommended that Canada focus its diplomacy on economic development and the defence of its national interests, which meant pushing peacekeeping and international mediation into the background. The white paper on defence, meanwhile, called for withdrawing half of all Canadian troops stationed in Europe and placing greater emphasis on national and continental defence. This new policy direction sparked a sharp reaction from none other than Pearson himself, the architect of Canadian multi-lateralism, who considered it "passive" and feared that it would result in Canada "disengaging" from the world scene.[5]

The new direction of foreign and defence policy pleased some

Canadian nationalists, but it was unrealistic. It took little notice of geographic realities (for example, Canada's one close neighbour, the United States) but also structural realities peculiar to Canada (the country's economic and military integration with the United States and Western countries). As a result, the American government regularly expressed annoyance over what it deemed the Canadian government's excessively nationalistic positions on the economy, as well as foreign policy initiatives it deemed anti-American.

Trudeau took note of these realities, quietly shunting the two policy papers to the sidelines. He no longer questioned Canada's membership in NATO and "gradually recovered several aspects of Pearson's internationalism."[6] For example, in 1983–1984, towards the end of his mandate, Trudeau embarked on an international peace initiative at a time when relations between the United States and the Soviet Union were quickly deteriorating. He undertook a world tour to promote nuclear disarmament and reduce tensions between East and West. He was unable, however, to make a dent in Canada's economic and military dependency on the United States. He even acquiesced to the testing of American cruise missiles in Canadian airspace. Besides, Canada became more dependent on trade with the United States during the Trudeau years, and Canada's new National Energy Program faced stern resistance in the central provinces and Washington alike.

Ultimately, Trudeau's new foreign and defence policy turned out to be a flop. According to two Canadian historians, Trudeau himself bore direct responsibility for this turn of events. He had "little long-term, consistent interest in foreign policy. When he came to power in 1968, he knew the world better than most leaders, but as a traveler not a student of foreign policy. His interest in defence matters in 1968, as in 1984, was non-existent; his interest in foreign policy was eclectic."[7] On the face of it, this judgment may seem harsh, but it is borne out by the reality that Trudeau devoted most of his energy to constitutional questions and the struggle against Quebec independence. He simply had no time to focus on foreign policy and defence the way Pearson had done in the early 1960s.

Even so, Pierre Trudeau charted two new policy directions that would eventually influence his son Justin. In October 1970, Canada became one of the first Western countries, along with France and the United Kingdom, to establish diplomatic relations with the People's Republic of China. This was a bold policy direction, considering the context of the early 1970s. It came two years before President Richard Nixon's visit to China.

A few years later, in 1976, Trudeau became one of the first Western heads of government to travel to Cuba on a state visit. On this occasion, Trudeau stirred up controversy by proclaiming, "*¡Viva Cuba! ¡Viva Castro!*" Twenty-four years later, Fidel Castro would be the only head of state to attend Pierre Trudeau's funeral in Montreal and to meet Justin Trudeau there. In 2016, Prime Minister Justin Trudeau travelled on state visits to China and Cuba, making a point of praising the regimes in power there. When Fidel Castro died, Justin Trudeau made an emotional and controversial tribute to "El Lider."

***

Justin Trudeau knew he had inherited a powerful family name. In his 2014 memoir, *Common Ground*, he describes his younger years, when he tried escaping the spotlight: "With all the new people I was meeting, it was a relief to sometimes not have to think about my last name and the effect it had on people when I first met them."[8]

Although Pierre Trudeau served as prime minister for sixteen years, he remained deeply unpopular from time to time and in various regions of the country. Starting in 1972, the popularity of the Liberal Party began collapsing in the four Western provinces, garnering only seven of the sixty-eight seats reserved for the West in the House of Commons. In 1979, the Liberals got just three seats in the Western provinces, losing power to a minority Conservative government. The problem was Western alienation at a time when political power in Ottawa was monopolized by representatives from Quebec and Ontario. Besides, Westerners disliked two policies that they felt Trudeau had imposed on them: official bilingualism and the National Energy Program. For many Westerners, the federal government was sucking up Western energy wealth and redistributing it to have-not provinces, mainly Quebec and the Maritimes.

In Quebec, people either loved or hated the prime minister. He won a string of overwhelming majorities in his home province, culminating in the 1980 election victory, when he won seventy-four of seventy-five seats. But a good part of the intellectual and political élite detested him — and not just supporters of Quebec independence. He was accused of being a centralizing politician and, even worse, of working against the interests of Quebec.

In his memoirs, Justin Trudeau barely alludes to his father's controversial reputation across Canada. The son was not particularly bothered by his father's reputation. Instead, he writes that he felt intimidated by his father's intellectual brio. He returns several times to this theme in the book. He admits that while pursuing studies at Collège Brébeuf (an upscale high school in Montreal) and McGill University, he was the opposite of his father. He showed "academic inconsistency."[9] He "fairly deliberately flunked Experimental Psychology," a prerequisite for getting into the McGill Faculty of Law, because he refused to follow in his father's footsteps.[10] "I had sabotaged that path, perhaps as a way of forcing myself, and my father, to come to grips with the fact that I would never be the academic high achiever he was."[11]

Despite this admission, Justin Trudeau's memoirs show that his relationship with his father troubled him. He devotes several pages to saying he knew he was smart, but not in the same way as his father.

Instead of law, Justin Trudeau studied English literature. When he got his bachelor's degree at the age of twenty-two, the shadow of his father reappeared. During a trip to France, he took some time to think about his situation and couldn't help drawing a parallel between himself and what his father had already achieved by that age. There was an intellectual gulf between father and son, and it hurt. He tried to find himself; the only way of doing this was to break away intellectually from his father. "I had already unhooked from [my father's] track, and my self-examination confirmed that a meandering path as a public intellectual was not for me."[12] He didn't see himself as either a future lawyer or a politician. Instead, he would become a teacher: "it would be my way of freeing myself from my family and our past."[13]

The rest is history. He did go into politics, just like his father. But before taking that step, he wanted to go on a round-the-world tour, just as his father had done after completing his studies. This would be Justin Trudeau's first real exposure to international affairs.

***

What did Justin Trudeau know about the world before setting off on this journey? In his childhood and youth, he accompanied his father on many jaunts abroad, although the experience often came down to government aircraft, official cars and hotels. He mainly met foreign heads of state and witnessed their interactions with his father. He drew a rather hasty conclusion: "[I]n foreign relations, relationships are vitally important."[14] He didn't give much more thought to the topic. He didn't recall the grim reality of national interests, forcing anyone exercising power to accept that states have no friends, only interests. This was exactly what went through Jean Chrétien's mind on his first meeting with George W. Bush: "Maybe he realized I wasn't going to be such a difficult guy to work with after all, despite all he might have heard from Brian Mulroney, and Canada–US relations were more important than our personal relations anyway."[15]

During this round-the-world trip, Justin Trudeau spent close to a year crisscrossing Europe, Africa and Asia, offering himself a taste of the customs and cultures of about fifteen countries and getting a better grasp of political and social issues shaking the planet.

He headed out in September 1994, accompanied by friends from Collège Brébeuf and a few others. The journey marked a turning point in his life, but he didn't seem to bring home many memories. In his memoirs, published twenty years later, he devotes a scant five pages out of 334 to his actual experiences on the trip. His account comes down to a series of commonplace remarks: "becoming terribly sick after eating leftover tuna salad" in Mauritania; visiting a village in Mali where he and his companions "were shown a tree under which, we were told, within living memory children had been sacrificed as part of religious ceremonies"; discovering "a presidential palace complete with crocodiles in a moat" in an unnamed country (Ivory Coast); having an image of the earth tattooed on his left shoulder in Thailand.[16]

He devotes one line to exploring Shanghai, Hong Kong, Hanoi and Bangkok, not referring to their history or social development. If anything, his descriptions reinforce the prejudices of certain readers about foreign places, particularly towards Africa. He makes dubious snap judgments without context: Wherever he goes, he finds societies consisting of a majority local population — the mainstream — and minorities viewed as "the others, an exception to the rule, to the national identity."[17] This leads him to an overall theory about the benefits of diversity. During the trip, he writes, "I had also had plenty of opportunities to observe that communities where people are open to difference, to others, are happier and more dynamic than places that are more insular and closed off."[18] Canada strikes him as the only country that has managed to strike a balance: "We have created instead a national identity that is based on shared values such as openness, respect, compassion, justice, equality, and opportunity."[19]

True, Canada is a tolerant land where the majority refuses to impose an exclusive definition of identity. But in his memoirs, Trudeau doesn't seem to remember that in the recent past, Canada was far from being the paradise he describes. The treatment of Indigenous peoples and of Canadians of Japanese origin during the Second World War are black marks in the country's history. Human rights have not always been so enthusiastically promoted. According to Canada's national mythology, the country is a leading advocate of human rights. But in 1948, Canada was the only country — outside of the Communist bloc — to abstain during the vote at the United Nations General Assembly on the final draft of the Universal Declaration of Human Rights.[20] Some Ottawa decision makers at the time held that freedom of expression, of religion and of association had no place in such a declaration. Canada ended up voting in favour only under the pressure of the American and British delegations, and would not start championing the cause of human rights until the 1960s.

On returning to Canada, Justin Trudeau got back into the daily grind. He completed his bachelor's degree in Education at the University of British Columbia and worked as a ski instructor, then as a commentator at a Montreal radio station. He kept out of sight, especially since his father still had a strong public presence. Then, suddenly, at Pierre Trudeau's funeral in 2000, Justin Trudeau stepped into the spotlight, stealing the scene. Broadcast around the world, the televised funeral attracted a crowd of glittering personalities, among them President Castro, former American president Jimmy Carter and the Aga Khan. Justin Trudeau gave an impressive eulogy for his father. Many commentators, noting his poise and presence, mused about whether he might go into politics. The former publisher of the Montreal newspaper *Le Devoir*, Claude Ryan, even wondered if this moment marked the birth of a dynasty.

But it was too soon to tell. Justin Trudeau let the dust settle until the Liberal Party of Canada's leadership convention in December 2006. He took part in the convention as a delegate, backing Stéphane Dion, who ultimately was voted in as leader. He found the convention a thrilling experience. He could see how popular he was, and he discovered he was good at politics, in a way completely unlike his father's intellectual approach to political activities. In fact, he liked everything his father hated: shaking hands, greeting crowds, socializing with people.[21]

After carefully thinking things over, Justin Trudeau was ready. In 2007, he was hoping to run in the riding of Outremont, where he lived, and let Stéphane Dion know. But the Liberal leader responded that he was planning to offer the riding to someone else.[22] So Trudeau turned to the Papineau riding, where Liberal supporters were few and far between. Dion, meanwhile, supported another candidate in the riding. But Trudeau was not one to give up easily. He worked hard and finally won the Liberal nomination there. He was elected as a member of Parliament during the 2008 election. He never forgot the cool reception he had received from Dion. Whatever his memoirs say, there was no love lost between the two men up to January 2017, when Trudeau fired Dion as minister of foreign affairs, a portfolio the latter had held since the 2015 election. I will return to this theme in chapter five.

***

Trudeau was thirty-six years old when he became the MP for Papineau, but he still wasn't ready to share his views on world affairs and Canada's place in the world. It is reasonable to ask whether he even had any such views, in spite of having "visited" a hundred countries before being elected.[23] By the time Stephen Harper was thirty-six, he had already articulated a position against the United Nations and multilateralism while advocating for a strong Canada that was more closely aligned with the United States. Trudeau's lack of interest in international affairs can be explained, to a certain extent. After the election, he became the Liberal critic for Youth, Higher Education, Amateur Sport, Multiculturalism, Citizenship and Immigration. These themes were not much in the news at the time. Between November 2008, when Justin Trudeau entered the House of Commons, and April 2011, when the general election was called, he put about thirty questions to the Conservative government, several of which had to do with Canada's intervention in Afghanistan.

Between election day in June 2011 and April 2013, when he became leader of the Liberal Party, Trudeau raised his profile during Question Period, putting about a hundred questions to the government in the House of Commons, but none of these questions involved foreign affairs.

He was just as reserved about foreign affairs during the Liberal leadership campaign. In a long speech announcing his leadership bid, he made a brief allusion to his future foreign policy: "We want a foreign policy that will give us hope in the future and that will offer solutions to the world."[24] He said little more than that in his acceptance speech upon becoming leader.

Between April 2013, when he became party leader, and the 2015 election, Trudeau made no trips abroad. He left it to other Liberals MPs to press the government on burning international issues, particularly on Canada's involvement in the alliance against the Islamic State in Iraq. Almost all of the approximately

300 questions the Liberal leader asked in the House of Commons had to do with domestic policies, which, it is true, were key to his own political destiny.

The people in Trudeau's inner circle were well aware of his weakness on international issues. With the approach of the next federal election, they naturally sought to strengthen his understanding of world affairs. The practice of fixed election dates meant that political parties enjoyed a period of stability and could more easily plan for the next election.

Trudeau's inner circle kept busy. At the beginning of 2014, they set up committees of experts and advisers who explored political, social and economic issues, generating the ideas that would form the core of the party's electoral platform. Ralph Lysyshyn, a former diplomat, joined the team as foreign policy adviser. Trudeau asked the Quebec MP Marc Garneau and the retired general and future MP Andrew Leslie to create an advisory council on foreign affairs whose mandate was to advise the Liberal leader on foreign and defence policy. I heard about this initiative and contacted Garneau, indicating that I would be interested in being on the council. The leader's office endorsed the choice. The council was set up in April 2014 and comprised nine experts specializing in different areas of foreign affairs, as well as five Liberal MPs. Seven members of Trudeau's inner circle also took part in our meetings. Several months later, Trudeau began seeking advice from Roland Paris, a brilliant professor of political science at the University of Ottawa who was an expert in peace and security issues. The team was now ready to give shape to Trudeau's foreign and defence policy.

CHAPTER TWO
THE EDUCATION OF A LEADER

When Justin Trudeau became Liberal Party leader in 2013, he wasn't particularly interested in international issues. Philosophically, he felt part of the great tradition of Canadian multilateralism that went back to Louis St. Laurent, Lester B. Pearson and John Diefenbaker, and continued under Pierre Trudeau, Brian Mulroney and Jean Chrétien. In a 2009 speech in the House of Commons, Trudeau said Canada had "a role as an international peacemaker."[1] Then, during his bid for the Liberal leadership in 2013, he added, "Canada must be a key player on the world scene, bringing forth positive debate and discussions."[2] He ventured to speak about China during the leadership campaign, but only from the point of view of economic relations between the two countries.[3] Doubtless, his views on foreign policy owed something to Pearson, but Trudeau's thinking had neither substance nor depth. He needed to get up to speed to flesh out these views. To do this, he worked closely with two diplomatic advisers and created the International Affairs Council of Advisors.

The Council comprised fourteen members — five MPs and nine experts — and held seven meetings with Trudeau and some of his inner circle between May 2014 and May 2015.[4] Each meeting lasted about two hours and allowed for frank and direct discussions among the Liberal leader and the Council members. The meetings addressed ten broad themes: multilateralism, defence spending, relations with the United States, Ukraine, conflicts in Africa, the Israeli–Palestinian peace process, development assistance, peacekeeping, military intervention against the Islamic State, and trade with China and India. Sometimes the invited experts submitted relevant notes or articles in advance, to make the discussions more fruitful.

Trudeau was particularly diligent. He always turned up on time and listened carefully to each of the presentations. He was there to learn. According to the minutes of the first five meetings, Trudeau remained unobtrusive and rarely intervened.[5] He had a good general understanding of the issues on the agenda, but he kept his questions and comments brief. He tended not to think outside the box and stuck to the foreign and defence policy dogmas Canada had maintained since 1945.

During the twelve months of the Council's existence, several international crises required his attention. Many crucial events took place on the world scene in 2014. Between January and March, the pro-Russian government of Ukraine was overthrown by opposition forces, with backing from the United States, Canada and Europe. Then Vladimir Putin responded harshly to what he considered foreign interference in the sphere of Russian influence. He annexed Crimea after a hasty referendum whose results were dubious. Putin directed a destabilization campaign in Ukraine, providing military and financial support to pro-Russian populations in the east of Ukraine.

At the same time, the emergence of the Islamic State (ISIS or Daesh), a new terrorist group in Iraq, then in Syria, led to an outbreak of violence in the Middle East. ISIS capitalized on political and religious conflicts in Iraq, a country destabilized by the tragic American invasion of 2003. ISIS spread into Sunni areas of the country, launching a reign of terror there, and proclaiming its objective of establishing a caliphate across the Arab-speaking world. ISIS seized opportunities during the civil war in Syria as well, extending its activities in that country. In August 2014, a coalition of Western and Arab countries bombed areas controlled by ISIS.

The Arab–Western intervention curbed the advance of ISIS on the ground, but the wars in Iraq and Syria led to an outpouring of refugees towards the neighbouring countries of Jordan, Lebanon and Turkey. The ISIS campaign of terror and subsequent coalition bombings aggravated the crisis, leading to a massive movement of refugees towards Western Europe. Within a few months, one million Syrians and Iraqis reached Greece, Germany and even the United Kingdom by land and sea. Germany welcomed several hundred thousand refugees; other countries were not as generous, taking in only a few thousand or even a few hundred refugees.

ISIS and terrorist movements like Al-Qaeda posed a direct threat to the West. These movements responded to coalition bombings in the Middle East by organizing and inspiring mass killings in Western countries. In September 2014, ISIS called on its supporters to kill Westerners wherever they were found, anywhere in the world. It specifically mentioned Canadians as potential targets. A month later, on October 20 and 22, 2014, two Canadians claiming to act in the name of Islamism killed two members of the Canadian Armed Forces, one in Saint-Jean-sur-Richelieu and one in Ottawa. One of the terrorists even managed to enter the federal Parliament, planning to kill MPs there. He was shot dead. On January 7, 2015, terrorists got into the newsroom of the satirical weekly *Charlie Hebdo* in Paris, murdering eleven people. This attack in particular led to an outpouring of public emotion: Forty-four heads of state and government led more than a million people in an anti-terror demonstration in Paris.

The International Affairs Council set an agenda of themes for deliberation. But the series of major emerging crises forced the

Council to juggle priorities constantly. On May 2 and August 26, 2014, many of the Council's deliberations focused on the crisis that had just erupted in Ukraine and the position Canada should adopt on Russia. I will return to this theme in a later chapter. The greater part of deliberations on September 22 and December 3 focused on ISIS.

Since the creation of the Arab–Western coalition against ISIS in August 2014, Canada had been involved only at a diplomatic level. But at the beginning of September, things suddenly changed. The Conservative government announced it was sending 100 military advisers to northern Iraq to assist Iraqi forces there. This mission was limited to thirty days, and still didn't involve directly taking part in combat.

The government's decision put the Liberals in a difficult position. They saw this initial commitment as a prelude to a tougher military intervention, which they opposed. At the same time, a majority of Canadians supported the Conservatives' proposal to launch air strikes. The Liberal Party feared that the use of force could split its own ranks. They had been sharply divided in the past on the use of force. Debates within the party sometimes spilled out onto the public square — even sparking a severe crisis in 1991, which played out on live television. As Canada got ready to participate that year in the multinational coalition to oust Iraqi troops from Kuwait, the Liberals, who were then the Opposition, took two sharply different positions in the House of Commons. The party leader at the time, Jean Chrétien, came out against Canada joining the coalition, while his fellow MP and rival, John Turner, supported Canada's involvement, as did several other Liberal MPs.

Twenty years later, the Liberal Party avoided publicizing any internal crisis. The debate on military intervention against ISIS was calmer. Some Liberal MPs, it is true, were ready to support bombing, but party debates took place within caucus and away from TV cameras. The International Affairs Council, made up of five Liberal MPs (Irwin Cotler, Kirsty Duncan, Mark Garneau, Ralph Goodale and Joyce Murray), along with retired general Andrew Leslie, came out against Canada's direct participation in combat. Instead, at the August 26, 2014, meeting, the Council came up with a proposal that differed from the Conservative one: the proposal called for Canada to offer humanitarian aid, transport local troops in Iraq, train Kurdish soldiers and welcome refugees to Canada. Trudeau also suggested highlighting Canadian expertise in building democratic institutions and especially in protecting the rights of minorities.

Several weeks later, on September 22, 2014, the members of the Council devoted an entire session to events in Iraq and Canadian involvement there. The Liberals were not against sending Canadian military advisers to northern Iraq, but insisted these advisers should not take on combat roles. For the purposes of debate, MP Marc Garneau asked Council members "if we would agree to support Canada's participation in air strikes." Nobody in the room showed any enthusiasm for the idea. On the contrary, one of the MPs present feared that the deployment announced by the Conservatives was no more than a prelude to Canada taking part in ground operations.

Trudeau was satisfied with the Liberal position. But he asked how the party should interpret the crisis in Iraq and Syria, taking into account key Liberal principles such as the Responsibility to Protect (R2P). This question was all the more compelling as information came to light on mass killings orchestrated by ISIS. R2P, a doctrine developed in 2001 by a committee created by the Chrétien government, spells out the serious human rights violations that oblige the international community to intervene. The key value underlying this doctrine is that national sovereignty can no longer serve as a bulwark behind which crimes can be committed with complete impunity. Even so, international intervention must be subject to many criteria before being triggered.

Ralph Lysyshyn, the Liberal leader's diplomatic adviser, and Roland Paris urged caution. They noted the doctrine was clear about the nature of human rights violations justifying the Responsibility to Protect. But the acts of violence apparently committed by ISIS were hard to substantiate. Trudeau knew how complex the situation was. He sought a way to defend the principles enshrined in R2P without using the wording specific to the concept. General Leslie proposed to the Council a more down-to-earth approach. He invited participants to study a proposal that was different from that of the Conservatives: deploying an armed humanitarian group composed of a medical unit, a company of engineers and two infantry companies for security, whose mission would be to save the lives of displaced persons or refugees in northern Iraq or Turkey. Trudeau warmed to the idea, but the Liberals didn't propose it in public.

Discussion then moved on to the question of Canada's possible air commitment against ISIS. Canada was about to be called on to take part in a bombing campaign, and Council members knew this commitment amounted to the combat role they opposed. They were soon proved right. On September 26, 2014, four days after the Council meeting, the United States asked Canada to take part in air raids. Prime Minister Harper agreed to the American proposal, putting the matter to debate and a vote in the House of Commons on October 8.

Trudeau got ready for the debate. A few days earlier, on October 2, he addressed Canada's air commitment at a meeting held by the think tank Canada 2020, on the theme "In 2020, what kind of country do we want to live in?" This venue provided Trudeau with an opportunity to stake out a position against the Conservative government's on a combat role for Canada against ISIS. The Liberal leader's close advisers wanted Trudeau to articulate a broader vision of Canada's role in conflicts.

The form and substance of the speech left a lot to be desired. The speech was rambling, lacked structure, and was abstract rather than concrete. The Liberal leader raised expectations with his opening words: "What is our role on the world stage? And how can we use our influence in a positive, constructive way?"[6] But he didn't make clear he was speaking only about Canada's role in the campaign against ISIS. Anyone in the audience hoping for a broader vision of Canada's role in international conflict was sorely disappointed.

Trudeau launched into a long diatribe against the Conservative government, which he accused of hiding its real intentions with respect to Canadian involvement in the coalition against ISIS. "Mr. Harper wants to go to war. He must tell us why,"[7] he said, recalling how in 2003 the United States had sought to gather international support for the war on Iraq under "false pretences." This time around, Canada had other ways to take part than sending "a handful of aging war planes."

The Liberal leader clearly rejected the United States government's request to provide Canadian CF-18s in the campaign: "Canada can play a significant role in Iraq, even if it does not undertake a combat role." He singled out "strategic airlift, training, or medical support" roles. He also suggested Canada's expertise in governance could help Iraq rebuild its institutions. Trudeau brought the speech to an end with a series of questions: "Who do we want to be? What are our values? What are our interests, and how do we want to pursue those interests in the world?" But he didn't answer these questions.

The speech had its shortcomings. But the Liberal leader managed to get across one key message: The Liberal Party opposed a combat role for Canada in Iraq. Liberal MPs stood firmly with him on the issue, voting on October 8 against the deployment of CF-18s in Iraq, and then, on March 31, 2015, against the expansion of air strikes to include Syria. During the December 3 meeting of the International Affairs Council, Trudeau and the Council members commended the party's position. Retired general Andrew Leslie summed up the feeling around the table when he said that as a soldier, he was proud Canada would not blindly comply with the request to send fighter jets to the Middle East.

Trudeau maintained this political line throughout 2015 and up to the October election. By sticking to the same message, he succeeded in rallying many Canadians around his humanitarian and moral approach to the victims of conflict. A tragic event that was bound to occur under the circumstances reinforced this conviction. On September 2, 2015, the lifeless body of a young Syrian boy of Kurdish descent washed up on the beach at a Turkish resort. The refugee crisis now had a human face. The press photo of the dead child went viral around the world, reopening the debate on the reception of refugees in Canada, right in the middle of an election campaign. The Conservatives offered to welcome a few thousand refugees, but Trudeau raised the stakes, promising to take in 25,000 refugees.

It is hard to say whether the Liberal leader's generous humanitarian stance contributed to his victory on October 19, 2015, but it certainly didn't hurt. It even strengthened the image of the future prime minister and of Canada on the international scene. After the election, media across the globe portrayed Trudeau and Canada as models of tolerance, openness and generosity in a world riddled with racism, distrust of others, and the oppression of minorities and immigrants.

***

In the eyes of Canadians and the international community, the military intervention against ISIS and the refugee crisis enabled the Liberal Party and its leader to stand out politically. During the election campaign, the Liberals invoked the moral imperative, which they saw as the basis of their political philosophy. With the approach of the October 2015 general election, they now sought to develop a foreign policy agenda reflecting this imperative as well as their vision of Canada in the world.

The person at the heart of this developing agenda was Roland Paris, a world-renowned expert in peace building and governance. Over the previous few years, he had worked at the Privy Council and the Ministry of Foreign Affairs, and was part of a committee of ten experts advising the NATO secretary general. His approach to international relations was rooted in the Canadian multilateral tradition since 1945. Up until the early 2010s, he wrote little about Canadian foreign policy. Then, in 2011, things started to change. In addition to his academic publications, Paris got involved in the public debate, writing opinion pieces for major English Canadian daily newspapers, mainly *The Globe and Mail*, and launching withering attacks on Stephen Harper's foreign policy. The time was right.

In October 2010, Canada failed for the first time since 1946 to be elected as a non-permanent member of the UN Security Council. Informed observers weren't particularly surprised that Canada should fail to obtain a seat on the Security Council. This was, after all, a direct consequence of Stephen Harper's policy of disengagement from world affairs, a policy he started implementing as soon as he gained power in 2006. The Conservatives were indifferent towards Africa, they were climate change skeptics and they took staunchly pro-Israeli positions. This attitude irritated many Arab and African countries. Even in Washington, the Obama administration no longer hid its exasperation over the Harper government's holier-than-thou approach and its stances on international issues.

Harper and the Conservatives hated the character of Canadian foreign policy consistently promoted by all governments since the end of the Second World War. The Conservative Party was the result of a merger between the Canadian Alliance (the former Reform Party) and the Progressive Conservative Party. Before assuming leadership of the "new" merged Conservative Party, Harper served as a Reform MP, then as leader of the right-wing party. Rooted in the Western provinces, Reformers were vehemently opposed to the concentration of power in the centre of the country, whether by Liberals or Progressive Conservatives. On foreign policy, the Reform Party rejected the "liberal internationalism" advocated by Canada's traditional parties.

Just after the Second World War, Canada's political and intellectual elites developed a philosophy of action for Canada on the world scene. This philosophy broke with isolationism, which combined an inward-looking attitude and hostility towards the international system. Instead, the philosophy embraced internationalism: According to this doctrine, interacting with the international community promoted world peace and stability, and therefore Canada's own prosperity and security. Internationalism was characterized by an active contribution to international institutions, multilateral diplomacy, disarmament efforts, peacekeeping operations, and the strengthening of the rules and norms of international law. This internationalism was liberal in the sense that it drew inspiration from a political philosophy promoting peace, democracy, freedom and justice. But this internationalism did not imply neutrality. Canada was a member of the Western bloc, through NATO and its military alliance with the United States within NORAD, the North American Aerospace Defense Command.

Reformers and then the "new" Conservatives rejected this idyllic vision, seeing it as out of sync with reality — at least their own. Shortly after Canada failed to get a seat on the UN Security Council, several Conservative ministers openly expressed their contempt for the United Nations, stating their intention of no longer going "along with some moral relativist crowd at the United Nations or elsewhere."[8]

Diplomacy being too soft and by nature relativist, Canada had to take on positions that were moral, virtuous and robust. Even before entering politics, Harper took this ideological stance. Recent history had helped Harper "form his Manichean view of the world: a black-and-white, right-or-wrong perspective," writes Mike Blanchfield, author of a book on the Conservative prime minister's foreign policy.[9]

Starting in 1997, Harper questioned foreign aid. He compared it to social security benefits, which only served to maintain the dependency of have-nots. Several years later, in 2002, in his first big foreign policy speech, Harper said relations with the United States was his sole priority.[10] A year later, during the American and British invasion of Iraq, Harper slammed Jean Chrétien's decision to stay out of the conflict, since it "betrayed Canada's history and its values."[11] But more was to come. In a letter co-authored with another Conservative leader and appearing in *The Wall Street Journal*, Harper told Americans that Canadians "stand with you."[12] He was no longer holding anything back. He blasted liberal elites for weakening and isolating Canada on the world scene. During the 2008 election campaign, five years after his famous opinion piece in *The Wall Street Journal*, Harper admitted during a televised debate that he regretted the position he had taken on the war in Iraq.

Despite these later qualms about Iraq, Harper never changed his basic message. In an interview with the weekly *Maclean's* magazine in 2011, he said that three founding principles of his Canada were "the courageous warrior, the compassionate neighbour, and the confident partner."[13] The interviewer asked why he had not chosen to say "a nation of peacekeepers, a nation of immigrants . . ." Were Canadians really accustomed to thinking of themselves as a warrior nation? Harper responded, "Well, not recently."

Harper wanted to deconstruct Canada's "liberal" identity, substituting something he felt was closer to the actual Canadian historical experience over the previous two centuries. The government therefore began removing references to events he found ideologically displeasing and replacing them with new ones. The monument to UN peacekeepers on the back of the $10 bill was replaced by a freight train. The War of 1812 replaced the First World War as a key event marking the emergence of Canadian nationhood and national identity. Parades marking the return of military personnel from overseas missions replaced Peacekeeping Day.

Roland Paris was clearly disturbed by Harper's vision of the world and of Canada's place on the international scene. He came out in public, accusing the prime minister of maintaining "a Manichean vision of international relations as a struggle between good and bad, and of moral clarity as the greatest asset and most reliable guide to foreign policy."[14] According to Paris, the Conservative government was uncomfortable with diplomacy. "Their default orientation is to divide the world into friends and enemies — white hats and black hats. When they are faced with competing imperatives and nuances, they seem to have difficulty calibrating their positions."[15] Harper took a particularly harsh position on the defence of human rights, which Paris judged to be selective and hypocritical.[16] According to Paris, "the government of Prime Minister Stephen Harper prides itself on having a principled foreign policy and for taking 'clear positions' in the defence of human rights," adding that Canada "barely utter[ed] a peep in public about Bahrain's terrible human rights record."

***

Roland Paris's bold positions shook up the little political world of Ottawa. They quickly came to Trudeau's attention: In fall 2014, his office contacted Paris, asking him to brief Trudeau regularly on foreign affairs. These briefings would run in parallel to Trudeau's meetings with the International Affairs Council. At the end of the year, Paris was mandated to draft a strategy to re-engage Canada on the international scene. He set to work, assembling a considerable number of documents, including the minutes of the Council, and meeting with a wide array of experts and people actively involved in international issues. In the lead-up to the October elections, his final strategy document served as basis for the foreign policy section of the Liberal Party platform.

Paris was a huge help to the Liberal leader. The clarity of his positions and the rigour of his demonstrations were immediately reflected in Trudeau's public statements. The Liberal leader's thinking became clearer, his words more refined. A speech Trudeau gave on Canadian–American relations on June 23, 2015, shows the extent of Paris's influence. I will return to this speech in chapter eleven. It was a far cry from the rambling and confused speech Trudeau had given a few months earlier on Canada's commitment to fighting ISIS.

While providing advice to the Liberal leader, Paris continued waging an intellectual battle in the media. In March 2015, he wrote a long open letter to "the 2015 federal election winner," drawing a not very flattering portrait of Canada's place on the international scene and recommending that the next prime minister "devise a foreign policy . . . for the future."[17] Paris sought to appear non-partisan, but in reading this article it is clear where his loyalties lay.

Over time, Paris became indispensable to Trudeau. He didn't hold any official position, but he could always be reached when the Liberal leader needed his advice. The day after the October 19 Liberal victory, Paris joined the transition team tasked with preparing the handover from the Harper government to the Trudeau government. On November 14, on the eve of Trudeau's departure for four international summits, the new prime minister named Paris senior political adviser for foreign affairs. Overnight, Paris found himself sitting beside the prime minister at meetings with United States president Barack Obama and Chinese president Xi Jinping.

One of his friends welcomed the choice of Paris as adviser: "If you have an eye for talent, this is one of the guys you're going to pick," the friend told the *National Post*.[18] And then, suddenly, everything fell apart. In June 2016, after just seven months, Paris resigned and headed back to his job as a professor at the University of Ottawa. The true reason for his departure is unknown, and Paris refuses to talk about it. Was he pressured into resigning, or did he leave his role as senior foreign affairs adviser voluntarily? Several theories about his sudden departure from government made the rounds. According to one view, the prime minister's inner circle had ostracized Paris, who had been an outsider from the beginning. Gerald Butts, Trudeau's senior political adviser until February 2019, had been a close friend of the prime minister's for over twenty years. Trudeau's chief of staff, Katie Telford, his director of communications, Kate Purchase, and a few others had all been Liberal activists and Trudeau supporters for more than a decade. They had been involved in all his struggles. Years in opposition had welded this group around the Liberal leader. Paris never managed to get into the inner circle. And this circle took no interest in issues of international politics and defence.

According to another theory, one that is harder to demonstrate, Paris proved incapable of "delivering the goods," as they say in the private offices of ministers. He thought more than he acted. In most offices on Parliament Hill, time is of the essence, and all eyes are on public opinion and the next election. Any programs that are developed necessarily include short-term deliverables. The objective is to tick boxes on a list and be able to show the electorate that government programs relating to women, youth, Indigenous people and the middle class were reaching their targets. Foreign policy and defence don't fit easily into this approach.

Sandwiched between Trudeau's inner circle, who avoided him, and the pressures of the policy development and implementation process, Paris understood he was less and less able to influence Trudeau. His time had passed.

PART 2
THE EXERCISE OF POWER

CHAPTER THREE
THE FIRST STEPS

The election campaign got under way in August 2015. The leaders of the three main parties geared up for a debate on foreign policy, to be hosted by the Munk School of Global Affairs and Public Policy at the University of Toronto on September 28. This televised debate would be the first of its kind in Canadian political and electoral history.

Trudeau was ready for the debate. The Liberal Party had just published its election platform, which included a dozen pages on foreign and defence policy, the fruit of debates and reflection throughout 2014–2015 by the members of the International Affairs Council and the Liberal leader's close advisers, including the academic Roland Paris.[1] Drawing on all this material, Paris had worked out a strategy of Canadian re-engagement on the world scene. This strategy served as the basis for foreign and defence policy commitments in the Liberal Party platform. Paris's ideas greatly influenced discussions at the Liberal leader's office: They went straight into the party platform. In a sense, Paris harkened back to the golden age of Canadian diplomacy in the 1950s and '60s, a time when Canada developed and promoted the philosophy of "liberal internationalism," grounded in active participation in the multilateral system, disarmament negotiations, peacekeeping operations and the strengthening of international law.

Paris blamed the Conservative government for abandoning this philosophy, which had long accounted for Canada's success on the international scene and had served its interests very well. "This liberal internationalism has been the non-partisan foundation of Canada's foreign policy at least since the Second World War," he noted in a blistering attack on Stephen Harper's foreign policy. "Working in multilateral institutions has historically given us a voice in international affairs that we would have otherwise lacked."[2]

Canada's prosperity depended on trade and the free movement of goods and people, so this philosophy helped strengthen an international system based on common rules, which in turn bolstered Canada's own stability. Paris stressed this philosophy in the advice he offered both to Trudeau and to the readers of his newspaper articles, because liberal internationalism still resonated with Canadian public opinion.

In a study published in fall 2014, Paris sought to determine whether the Harper government's public discourse and policies on Canada's role in the world since 2006 had changed Canadian attitudes: In short, did Canadians still support liberal internationalism, or did they prefer the Harper government's more robust foreign policy?[3] Paris brought together the results of opinion polls and surveys over a long time frame to measure variations in public opinion on particular foreign policy themes.

The study's conclusions were crystal clear: Canadians remained deeply attached to United Nations peacekeeping, multilateralism and foreign aid. Paris concluded that the Conservatives had failed to change Canadian behaviour. More than that, the study revealed that the Conservative Party's strategy of attracting new Canadians, a majority of whom came from countries with traditional and authoritarian values, was a flop. The data showed Harper's charm offensive wasn't working. New Canadians were just as committed as long-time Canadians to the values of liberal internationalism. From an electoral point of view, the Liberal Party had a good prospect of gaining votes in culturally diverse communities.

The Liberal Party platform reflected the conclusions Paris had reached in his study. The vocabulary of liberal internationalism featured prominently in the dozen pages of the platform devoted to foreign and defence policy: A Trudeau government would "restore Canadian leadership in the world . . . renew and repair relationships" with the United States and the international community; "refocus our development assistance on helping the poorest and most vulnerable . . . renew Canada's commitment to peacekeeping operations . . . provide support during natural disasters, humanitarian support missions, and peace operations"; respond to "the suffering" of refugees, demonstrating openness towards them and welcoming them to Canada. A Liberal government would deliver on this platform by implementing "compassionate" and "humane" policies and programs. The Liberal Party platform was a triumph of what Americans call soft power, as opposed to the hard power valued by Stephen Harper and the Conservatives.

***

The TV debate on September 28 was an important opportunity for all three party leaders. Trudeau's performance attracted attention. He conveyed emotion, which appealed to many of the 3,000 people in the audience. He spoke with passion about the tragedy of the Syrian refugees and about the Conservative government's lack of generosity. After ten years in power, Harper seemed on the defensive and sustained repeated attacks on his record. His two opponents accused him of weakening Canada on the international scene and of neglecting Canada's all-important relationship with the United States.

Thomas Mulcair wasn't comfortable with international issues, so he focused his attacks directly on Trudeau himself. He was biting and sarcastic towards the Liberal leader, repeatedly referring to him as "Justin" and wondering how he could ever stand up to the Vladimir Putins of the world. Each time, Trudeau provided masterful, quick-fire responses. Clearly, his seven briefings with the International Affairs Council and one-on-one meetings with top advisers like Paris had served him well.

***

On October 19, 2015, the Liberal Party won a solid majority after one of the longest election campaigns in Canadian history. For some observers, this victory came as a surprise. Initially, the New Democrats led the opinion polls, ahead of the scandal-ridden Conservative Party. Stephen Harper had expected that a long campaign would ultimately serve his interests, focusing the attention of voters not on his government's failings but on its economic and social record.

The Liberal Party, meanwhile, had started the election campaign in third place. Over the campaign, however, support for the Liberals slowly inched upwards. Trudeau took risks, announcing that his future government was ready to increase the deficit to stimulate the economy. Also, he was ready to welcome tens of thousands of Syrian refugees. His stance on the refugee issue was bold, considering that it came at a time when public opinion, in Canada as well as in other Western countries, was hostile towards immigration policies and the reception of refugees.

The televised leaders' debates revealed something paradoxical. NDP leader Thomas Mulcair, a social democrat by conviction, seemed overly cautious on many issues. His tax plan was quite close to Harper's. For his part, Trudeau openly embraced government spending as a way of stimulating growth.

Canadians faced confusing political choices. Opinion polls suggested voters were volatile and wanted change. By and large, Canadians didn't trust the NDP to run the country and fretted about Trudeau's lack of experience. At the same time, they knew Trudeau was leader of a political party that had governed Canada almost continuously during the twentieth century. Towards the end of the campaign, the winds of change swept across the country. The Liberal Party broke away from the pack and settled into first place, leaving the NDP, initially the front runner, to slip into third place.

***

At the beginning of November 2015, a few days after the Liberals were sworn in as the new government, Trudeau and some of his ministers headed to the Lester B. Pearson Building, which houses the Ministry of Foreign Affairs. Hundreds of government workers congregated in the lobby dominated by a huge portrait of Queen Elizabeth II. They knew Trudeau was on his way, and the place was buzzing. Here was the prime minister now. There was a sudden flurry of activity as civil servants rushed up to him, shook his hand, took photographs and applauded. This previously unheard-of reception was happening for good reason: Several hours earlier, Trudeau had sent a letter to all leaders of missions abroad announcing he was lifting the gag order the Conservatives had imposed on them. The prime minister now invited them to speak about Canada's role in the world as part of their regular duties. He also called on them to share their experience and expertise with the new members of his government.

This letter made the rounds in Ottawa, reaching well beyond diplomatic circles. All civil servants felt it directly affected them. Scientists working on environmental issues were particularly happy with this decision, because for the past decade, the

Conservatives had forbidden them from sharing any research findings with the media.

Two days after the prime minister's visit, foreign affairs employees removed the portrait of the Queen and put up two paintings by the famous Canadian artist Alfred Pellan, which the Conservatives had taken down four years earlier. Let there be no doubt about it: Ottawa had a new government.

***

The civil servants and diplomats at foreign affairs weren't the only ones to welcome the new government with open arms. International public opinion swooned over the prime minister. Trudeau's remarks on diversity, tolerance and openness were a breath of fresh air at a time when part of the electorate in Europe and the United States were rejecting the traditional parties and embracing populism instead. For some, it was hard to distinguish between Islamic terrorism and waves of migrants. These phenomena caused deep social tensions and led to hate speech and xenophobia.

On these questions, Trudeau stood out. Although barely elected to office, the prime minister became the focus of a personality cult. Several leading international magazines put him on the front cover, alone or with his wife, Sophie Grégoire. The French weekly *Le Point* showed the prime minister jogging in Ottawa, with the heading "Trudeau, the antidote to Trump." The American fashion magazine *Vogue* published a sensual photo of Trudeau hugging his wife. Two years later, in Summer 2017, *Rolling Stone* magazine put a new spin on Trudeaumania, featuring the prime minister on its cover and asking, "Why Can't He Be Our President?" The story inside continued: "Is he the free world's best hope?"

"All that is excessive is insignificant," said the great French diplomat Talleyrand two centuries ago. Maybe Talleyrand was right, but it seemed as if part of the world had succumbed to Trudeau's charms, while some Americans, dismayed by Donald Trump's election as president a year later, found in Trudeau a counter-model to Trump.

Trudeau recognized the extent of his international popularity. At the beginning of November 2015, nine days after being sworn in, he headed off on a month-long diplomatic marathon involving stopovers on two continents and attendance at four world summits. Canadian Press reporter Mike Blanchfield has described the reception Trudeau got at these international meetings.[4]

Trudeau stopped first in Turkey to attend the G20 summit, where he met the leaders of nineteen other great economic powers. He was on unfamiliar ground and had no direct experience of the exercise of power or of international summits. In any case, the young novice managed to break the ice. In Ankara, he got laughs from the other leaders by saying, "This summit is, by far, the best one I have ever attended."[5] A few days later, he was in Manila, the Philippines, at the APEC summit of the of Asia-Pacific countries. He got rock star attention as a frenzied crowd ran after him, shouting his name. A local newspaper dubbed him the sexiest leader at the summit, along with the Mexican president. After this he headed to Malta, in the Mediterranean, for the Commonwealth Summit, and then, finally, to Paris on November 28, 2015, for a conference on climate change. While in Paris, he paid his respects at the Bataclan concert hall, in the centre of the city, where Islamist terrorists had slaughtered a hundred people just a few days before.

Everywhere Trudeau went, he communicated a message of hope and optimism. And he used his reputation and public image to promote Canada. "If you are looking for a country that has the diversity, the resilience, the positivity and the confidence that will not just manage this change but take advantage of it, there has never been a better time to look to Canada," he said at the World Economic Forum in Davos, Switzerland, in January 2016.[6]

***

Trudeau had to assemble his Cabinet right after the election. It was a huge challenge. The Liberals had gone from thirty-four to 184 MPs in the House of Commons. Trudeau had to choose his Cabinet ministers from this large group, while striking a balance between men and women, the different provinces, urban centres and the regions, Canada's two main language groups, cultural and community representation, Indigenous peoples and people with disabilities. Finally, he had to reward MPs who had remained loyal to him through years in opposition. The team of ministers responsible for foreign and military policy brought together veterans and novices, representatives of diverse cultural communities and experienced individuals.

Stéphane Dion, a Montreal-area MP, led this group. Dion was a former minister under the Chrétien and Martin governments, a former Liberal leader and former Leader of the Official Opposition. He was a seasoned politician and formidable parliamentarian. Trudeau named him to Foreign Affairs, the most prestigious position in the Cabinet. Trudeau named two junior ministers to assist Dion: Toronto-area MP Chrystia Freeland as minister of international trade, and Sherbrooke MP Marie-Claude Bibeau as minister of international development and La Francophonie. Trudeau named Harjit Sajjan — a former Canadian Army officer, a Sikh born in India and a veteran of the war in Afghanistan — to the position of minister of national defence. Finally, Kent Hehr, an Alberta MP who is a lawyer and a paraplegic, was named minister of veterans affairs. Trudeau was now ready to assume the reins of leadership and to tackle international issues head-on.

CHAPTER FOUR
STÉPHANE DION TAKES OVER

When Stéphane Dion was appointed minister of foreign affairs in November 2015, he was already well known on the national political scene. He was a professor of political science at the Université de Montréal, and like Justin Trudeau was the son of someone famous. His father, Léon Dion, was one of Canada's leading political scientists. Stéphane Dion was interested in Quebec and Canadian politics, but he mostly taught public administration and the analysis of organizations.

When he began teaching in 1984, I was starting my master's degree at the Université de Montréal. I had never met him before. He didn't cut a flamboyant figure, but we students knew he was strict and demanding.

Dion took part in the constitutional debate during the 1995 referendum campaign. In radio and television interviews as well as opinion pieces in the major daily newspapers, he countered the arguments of independence supporters. He was one of Quebec's rare intellectuals to come out swinging in public with a combination of rational and emotional arguments in favour of Canada. The extremely narrow victory for the "No" side on October 30 sent shock waves through the federalist camp. A plan of action was urgently needed, or the pro-independence camp might win the next referendum.

For this reason, Prime Minister Jean Chrétien decided to shuffle his Cabinet. He wanted to inject some fresh blood from Quebec. Who better than Dion? In Chrétien's memoirs of his time as prime minister, he recounts how one evening in November 1995, while watching television, his wife, Aline, pointed out how well Stéphane Dion was performing in a debate. At first, Chrétien was skeptical. He didn't see a university professor as a good fit for Cabinet. "The problem with professors in power," he writes, "is that they tend to place their abstract ideas ahead of practical consequences in order to prove some theory or other."[1] But he was impressed by Dion's performance on television. "The more I watched, the more I became as impressed as Aline had been by his firm, intelligent defence of Canadian federalism."[2]

Chrétien phoned him. At first, Dion thought this had to be some kind of student prank. A few hours later he was in Ottawa, at the prime minister's official residence. Chrétien offered him the post of minister of intergovernmental affairs, responsible for national unity. But Dion wasn't even a member of Parliament. After thinking it over for a few weeks, he accepted.

As a freshly appointed minister, his enthusiasm and combative spirit made waves. He piloted the Clarity Act through Parliament — a significant achievement, since it set conditions for any province seeking to separate from the rest of Canada. Once Chrétien retired from politics in December 2003, Dion continued working with the new prime minister, Paul Martin, who appointed him minister of the environment a few months later. In 2005, at a United Nations conference on climate change in Montreal, Dion managed to develop an international consensus in the fight to reduce greenhouse gas emissions. Even environmentalists were impressed.

A year later, voters turfed the Liberals out of office, Martin resigned and after a tough leadership campaign to replace him, Dion was voted in as Liberal Party leader at the end of 2006. This meant Dion automatically became Leader of the Opposition. He led the Liberals to defeat in the 2008 elections and had to step down as leader.

***

After a brilliant academic, parliamentary and ministerial career, Dion's appointment as minister of foreign affairs in 2015 was his crowning achievement. It meant his abilities were being recognized. It also meant he was being rewarded. During the election campaign, Trudeau articulated his foreign policy priorities around the theme "Canada is back." His program focused on peace, multilateralism, combating climate change, diversity and the defence of human rights. Trudeau was therefore on the lookout for a Liberal MP with the intellectual stature needed to help restore Canada's credibility on the international scene after nine years of Conservative rule.

At the same time, being minister of foreign affairs meant holding one of the top Cabinet posts after the prime minister himself. This post is seen as a reward for loyal service to the government, or for a steady and brilliant performance on the Opposition benches. Unless, of course, the prime minister wanted to appoint a self-effacing person who would quietly do the grunt work of foreign affairs abroad, while leaving the PM to get all the public accolades at home. Stephen Harper appointed six successive ministers to this post during his nine years of power, none of whom left a mark on international issues.

Dion certainly had intellectual stature, and he demonstrated unflinching political loyalty. His track record under Chrétien and Martin was beyond reproach, and he had served well as an Opposition MP. In fact, Dion was a natural choice for Trudeau as minister of foreign affairs. This wasn't the first time a prime minister chose a former party leader for this position. Brian

Mulroney gave the portfolio to Joe Clark in 1984, after beating him in the Conservative leadership campaign. Clark stayed in the role for seven years.

Dion was sworn in on November 4, 2015, and was immediately thrust into the thick of things. He had only a few days to get ready to accompany the prime minister to four high-stakes international meetings that had been planned long before: the G20 summit in Turkey, the APEC summit in the Philippines, the Commonwealth summit in Malta and the Paris climate change conference.

As minister, Dion had no chief of staff, no director of communications, no political adviser. He relied on a small team to liaise with the civil servants at Foreign Affairs; the team organized briefing sessions between the minister's office and the civil servants responsible for particular files. Dion knew the system. He was a pro. He knew how a ministry functioned and he quickly got down to work. He read day and night. Meanwhile, the Prime Minister's Office found him a chief of staff, tasked with recruiting the political staff for the minister's office and supporting them in their work.

***

The minister of foreign affairs runs an enormous team of several thousand diplomats and civil servants stationed in Ottawa and spread out in about 200 diplomatic posts abroad. Some of these employees are responsible for the daily management of government policies in international relations. These diplomats and civil servants develop policies, prepare files and discuss international issues with other ministries concerned — National Defence, International Development and La Francophonie, Immigration, Public Safety, Environment. They also represent Canada in all foreign countries and in international organizations, and interact with NGOs and civil society. These diplomats and civil servants maintain institutional memory: They remind each incoming government of Canada's traditional positions on a broad range of international issues.

Being minister of foreign affairs is a back-breaking job, and one that is often misunderstood by the media and the general public. The minister has to make the best of things if he wants to reach government targets. He needs to surround himself with a strong team that serves both to drive policy through a process and to filter relations between the minister and the massive governmental machine.

Dion was not a foreign policy expert. On the advice of his chief of staff, he chose six advisers to provide the best guidance on the most important foreign affairs files and to work with him to generate new ideas. On November 7, 2015, three days after Dion was sworn in as minister, I contacted him, indicating my interest in joining his staff. He suggested I phone his chief of staff and send my CV. I started in Dion's office on February 22, 2016, tasked with multilateralism, peacekeeping operations and Africa.[3] I also wrote the speeches he would give in French.[4] Foreign Affairs was familiar territory for me. I had known Dion for many years and I knew the ministry well.

***

I first met Stéphane Dion at the end of the 1980s at a book launch he attended with his wife, Janine Krieber, who was then a professor at the French-language Royal Military College in Saint-Jean-sur-Richelieu, near Montreal. We kept in touch periodically. In January 2007, Jean Lapierre, Liberal MP for Outremont, resigned. Dion had been party leader for a few months; I contacted him, indicating my interest in running for the Liberals in Outremont. He didn't say no, but he waited until

July before appointing me as Liberal candidate in a by-election in the riding, to be held on September 17. The Conservatives had no chance of taking Outremont. The New Democratic Party was then virtually unknown in Quebec, but NDP leader Jack Layton was popular across Canada. As candidate for Outremont, Layton recruited Thomas Mulcair, a Quebec political heavyweight. The by-election campaign got quietly under way. Outremont had once been a safe seat for the Liberals, but in 2006 they managed to get only 36 per cent of the votes, with the Bloc Québécois close on their heels at 30 per cent. Justin Trudeau came twice to the riding to support my campaign. Each time, crowds jostled around him, fans straining to have their picture taken with him, even though he made a point of introducing me. It didn't make any difference. Here was the new Trudeaumania, happening under my very eyes. But on election night, we had to face reality: The winds of change propelled Mulcair to victory, with some strategic help from Bloc Québécois supporters.

I kept in touch with Dion and the Liberal Party in the years that followed. In April 2014, I joined Trudeau's International Affairs Council, which gave me the chance to meet Dion more frequently and to promote my ideas for Africa, peacekeeping and multilateralism.

I knew the ministry well. Starting in 1985, I got to know dozens if not hundreds of diplomats and civil servants at Foreign Affairs, and I maintained these relationships for thirty years, first as a journalist at the Montreal daily *Le Devoir*, then as director of the Montreal office of the Pearson Peacekeeping Centre, and finally as director of the French-speaking research network on peace operations that I founded at the Université de Montréal. These relationships served me well.

While working in the minister's office, I crossed paths daily with acquaintances in the corridors of the ministry or during one of our missions abroad. This proximity made a big difference when I needed to discuss particular issues with civil servants. Officially, the political staff in the minister's office is only supposed to contact civil servants via the Liaison Branch. This is a way of preventing political staff from exerting direct influence on them. But in reality, a political adviser can speak with a civil servant any time they bump into each other in the ministry elevator or cafeteria. I never hesitated to tap my network at the ministry to push files forward.

***

During the election campaign, Trudeau promised to make Canada a constructive and key player on the international scene. And right after the election, the new prime minister told our foreign interlocutors that Canada was back. There was a flurry of diplomatic activity as relations were relaunched with the United States, new overtures were made to Russia and Iran, and moves were made to heighten security in the Arctic, protect the environment, participate in UN peacekeeping operations, change the tone of Canada's approach to the conflict between Israel and Palestine, propose new lines of action on disarmament, deepen our relationship with China, reassure countries in Eastern Europe of NATO's determination to guarantee their security with regard to Russia, and reformulate Canada's involvement in operations against the Islamic State in Iraq and Syria.

Dion was there to give substance to this program of activity. Like most politicians in Ottawa, he believed in "liberal internationalism." Dion had been steeped in this ideological environment ever since his studies in political science at Université Laval. As a minister in the Chrétien and Martin governments, he saw how much this political principle benefited Canada and the world.

At the time, Lloyd Axworthy, as minister of foreign affairs, was the one to bring liberal internationalism back to the fore.

He popularized the concept of human security developed by the UN, a concept based on individuals and their security.[5] Accordingly, Canada proposed a series of measures to the international community, aimed at reinforcing the protection of human rights and the security of individuals. In 1997 and 1998, a majority of UN member states ratified the Ottawa Convention on the Prohibition of Anti-Personnel Mines as well as the treaty creating the International Criminal Court, whose mandate was to prosecute persons accused of genocide, war crimes and crimes against humanity.

In 2001, Canada championed the Responsibility to Protect, a principle that, although without legal force, reminded the international community it could and sometimes had to intervene to punish massive human rights violations committed by states unable or unwilling to do so themselves. In 2003, Canada also refused to take part in the American and British joint military campaign against Iraq without prior authorization from the UN Security Council.

Dion was part of this tradition. The Conservatives had abandoned the ideals of liberal internationalism during their nine years in power. Now the minister wanted to revive this principle and adjust it to new international realities. The world had undergone a lot of changes since Axworthy's time. The September 11, 2001, terror attacks revealed that powerful and well-organized Islamist terrorist groups could strike anywhere on the planet, at any time. China was emerging as a new superpower. Russia at times resorted to brute force to regain its status as a great power. Western military interventions in Afghanistan, Iraq and Libya didn't provide the hoped-for results, and even seemed to have worsened the situation in the three countries concerned. Whole regions of Africa and the Middle East were wracked by economic problems, a lack of democracy and escalating religious, ethnic and identity-driven strife, which caused instability and the greatest migrations of populations since the end of the Second World War. In the West, the rise of populism threatened the very foundations of liberal democracy.

As the new minister, Dion was worried about this challenging international context. We often discussed it together while preparing his speeches. He wanted Canadian diplomacy to address factors liable to contribute to anxiety and war, and in so doing make Canada a determined architect of peace.

Dion also wanted to enable Canada to navigate this new international environment. He worked out a general philosophical approach, an ethical position to support the government's actions, make them more acceptable to Canadians and more effective in the wider world. This meant continuing a long-established tradition of Canadian leadership: grounding actions in ethics and the liberal internationalist promotion of justice, democracy and freedom.

In his day, Pierre Trudeau often spoke about ethics. The former prime minister sought a world where the actions of states and their leaders were grounded in ethical rules. He worried about the widening gap between North and South, between the phenomenal wealth of industrial countries and the daily struggle for survival of people in developing countries. For this reason, at two conferences in the United States and the United Kingdom, he called on the international community in 1974 and 1975 to adopt a "new ethic of broad responsibility"[6] towards the poorest of the poor — this ethics "abhors the present imbalance in the basic human condition."[7] Throughout his term in office, he invested heavily in development assistance and put himself heart and soul into bringing North and South together.

Forty years later, Dion took up the same cause, finding inspiration in the thought of the German sociologist Max Weber.

Weber's writing covered several fields of human activity. He was particularly interested in political action. In *Politics as a*

Vocation, he sought to develop an ethical approach to support political action, which ultimately concerned conflict between individuals and nations. But Weber noted there is no single fundamental unifying principle, because

> *"We must be clear about the fact that all ethically oriented conduct may be guided by one of two fundamentally differing and irreconcilably opposed maxims: conduct can be oriented to an 'ethic of conviction' or to an 'ethic of responsibility.' This is not to say that an ethic of conviction is identical with irresponsibility, or that an ethic of responsibility is identical with unprincipled opportunism. Naturally nobody says that. However, there is an abysmal contrast between conduct that follows the maxim of an ethic of conviction — that is, in religious terms, 'The Christian does rightly and leaves the results with the Lord' — and conduct that follows the maxim of an ethic of responsibility, in which case one has to give an account of the foreseeable results of one's action."[8]*

In other words, people favouring the ethic of conviction seek to impose a doctrine without regard to practical consequences, whereas those favouring the ethic of responsibility adjust to reality and accept responsibility for their actions.

But is it possible to reconcile the differing attitudes that people take when interacting with the world? As someone grounded intellectually in Weber's thought, Dion hesitated. In January 2016, in one of his first speeches as minister of foreign affairs, he drew a distinction between the two ethical approaches: "[P]olitical leaders should be guided by the ethics of responsibility, as opposed to the ethics of conviction."[9]

In March 2016, two months later, he said it was possible to blend these two ethical approaches in developing a guiding principle for political action. He outlined this thinking in a speech before a panel of jurists at the University of Ottawa. This was the first time the minister unveiled the government's guidelines on foreign policy, and he paid great attention to detail while giving the guidelines a solid intellectual foundation. He asked me to reread the part of Weber's *Politics as a Vocation* devoted to the two ethical approaches and to write a first draft of the speech, incorporating aspects of our policy concerning Russia, Iran and the sales of military vehicles to Saudi Arabia. The speech took a few days to take shape, as it passed from one desk at Foreign Affairs to the next. Finally, the day before the conference, everything was ready.

According to Dion, "Max Weber did not claim that those who support the ethics of responsibility lack conviction. But since this is how he is often misinterpreted, I prefer to go beyond his rigid distinction to create a more syncretic concept — the ethics of 'responsible conviction.' This formulation means that my values and convictions include the sense of responsibility. Not considering the consequences of my words and actions on others would be contrary to my convictions."[10] The concept recalls the importance of convictions in all political undertakings, combined with a sense of responsibility, without which nothing is possible in this world. It applies to both national and international affairs.

But does the principle of "responsible conviction" serve to justify the unjustifiable? This was not a purely theoretical question. A few months before the Conservatives were defeated, they authorized the sale of armoured vehicles to Saudi Arabia, which has one of the world's worst human rights records. During the election campaign, the three main parties all promised to respect the $15-billion contract.

But Canadian law is very clear about the export of weapons to countries suspected of violating human rights: The Canadian government reserves the right to cancel a weapons sales contract if it can be demonstrated that the weapons are being used in military operations where human rights are violated.

As a result, the new Liberal government issued export certificates for the sale of the armoured vehicles in the belief they would not be used to suppress the population. According to Dion, the contract met the criteria of "responsible conviction." Dion maintained that responsible conviction must not be confused with "some sort of moral relativism." On the contrary, this principle enabled Canada to better formulate its foreign policy by taking into account morality as well as economic and geopolitical interests.

Dion also invoked the principle of responsible conviction to leverage diplomatic commitment and reach his objective of making Canada an architect of peace. He rejected the politics of isolation. "It is often a mistake to sever all ties with a regime that we dislike," he said. "On the contrary, we must speak to such regimes frankly, and clearly express our convictions, with a view to effecting positive change."

He pointed to the example of relations between Canada and the Soviet Union in the 1980s. With Harper's politics of disengagement, said Dion, "it would have been impossible to invite a young Mikhail Gorbachev to Canada in 1983." But "it was in Ontario and Alberta that Gorbachev first came to see the great inefficiencies of the Soviet agricultural system compared to ours." Dion also cited the example of Cuba. In one of his last speeches, just after the death of Fidel Castro, he spoke about the situation in Cuba while enthusiastically defending the policy of engagement followed by all Canadian governments there since the 1959 Revolution. The policy of "constructive engagement" towards Cuba, Dion told the House of Commons, enabled Canada to be "an influential and trusted voice that can push to move Cuba further in the direction of reform, both economic and political."[11]

Dion's advocacy of dialogue and his opposition to isolation were in line with all foreign policy implemented by all Canadian governments since 1945, with the exception of the Harper government. Many examples can be cited. Lester B. Pearson was Secretary of State for External Affairs at the time of the Korean War of 1950–1953. He was deeply concerned that the stark opposition of Soviet and American camps in that theatre could destroy the multilateral system. "It was critical, in Pearson's view, to keep the United States in the UN and the UN in the United States; it was also important to keep the Soviet Union in the UN."[12]

The Conservative Prime Minister John Diefenbaker took the same position on apartheid in South Africa, which was splitting the Commonwealth right down the middle. He succeeded in closing the gap "between African and Asian members, on the one hand, and the United Kingdom, Australia and New Zealand, on the other," thus preventing the Commonwealth from bursting apart.[13]

***

Canada is widely recognized as a middle power in the international system. This geopolitical status results from the country's economic, social and diplomatic development since the beginning of the twentieth century. This status was reinforced over the course of the century, through trade with the British Empire and then with the United States, the absence of conflict, the settlement of Canada due to successive waves of educated and industrious immigrants, and the decision to engage in the world community through multilateralism. The only way of maintaining this status is to engage in very active diplomacy.

"One of the main characteristics of middle powers is that they tend to adopt positions that strengthen the stability of the international system, which they view as vital for their prosperity and their security," write experts on international relations.[14] This is all the more important for Canada, which is sandwiched between the United States to the south and the Soviet Union (now Russia) to the north. All diplomatic initiatives launched by Lester B. Pearson, John Diefenbaker, Pierre Trudeau, Brian Mulroney and Jean Chrétien since 1945 sought to reduce or solve conflicts between East and West. But these initiatives also sought to solve conflicts within the Western bloc itself: for example, during the Suez Crisis of 1956, which pitted France and the United Kingdom on one side, against the United States and Canada on the other.

How could the new Liberal government reconnect with this Canadian tradition as an architect of peace after nine years of Conservative rule had sharply broken with it? Dion addressed this question in two major speeches in Quebec City and Montreal in May and October 2016. He was on solid ground; Canadians remained committed to the United Nations, peacekeeping and diplomacy, as the fall 2014 public opinion survey published by Roland Paris clearly showed.[15]

In Quebec City, Dion addressed a panel of former ministers of foreign affairs, academics, researchers and students, making an assessment of the current international situation. "We must not lose sight of the progress being made," he said.[16] He cited a number of success stories: the nuclear agreement between Iran and the international community, warming diplomatic relations between Washington and Havana, the restoration of democracy in Myanmar and Tunisia, the Paris Agreement on Climate Change. These were signs of hope. But there remained significant challenges.

The minister noted three kinds of threats. The first consisted of "classic geopolitical conflicts, linked to territorial and resource aspirations and to the clash of national ambitions." The second was what Dion called the "syndrome of mistrust." It consisted of "communities and populations that have lived peacefully side by side . . . [that] have come to fear, hate and attack each other . . . When neighbours and refugees or other foreigners are marginalized or persecuted because of political, religious, ethnic or racial differences, all the ingredients are in place to exacerbate mistrust and provoke an explosion." Evidence of this threat was there for all to see in Darfur, Mali, Afghanistan and Yemen. Finally, the third threat was "the state of crisis in which our ecosystems find themselves. Climate change and access to potable water are the most pressing manifestations of this crisis."

Canada could not ignore these tensions, threats or conflicts. Canada even had a special responsibility regarding the syndrome of mistrust, due to the country's own history, culture and diversity. "Canada's responsibility . . . is to demonstrate, in word and deed, that diversity must be considered an asset to humanity, not a threat . . . We must be the champions of diversity," he told the audience.

A few months later, Dion gave a speech in Montreal, providing more detail about how Canada planned to help the international community achieve world peace. In the speech, he stressed the government's determination to re-engage in UN peacekeeping operations.[17] These operations were a vital tool for the international community in the management and resolution of conflicts around the world, and they had a human face: the Blue Helmets, which Lester Pearson came up with for the United Nations during the Suez Crisis of 1956. The United Nations was crucial to Canada's involvement in the system of international security, along with Canada's military, political and economic alliance with the United States and its membership in NATO.

UN peacekeepers had been a key feature of Canadian

identity for a long time, and Canadians continued supporting them, as the study by Roland Paris showed.[18] The Liberals were well aware of this. In August 2016, a few weeks before Dion's speech in Montreal, the government unveiled its policy of re-engagement with peacekeeping operations. I contributed to the reflections on the subject as well as to the subsequent drafting of policy, which was meant to address the new realities of conflicts. Whereas peacekeeping in Pearson's day had involved stationing UN troops in between two states in conflict, the early twenty-first century called for interventions within states themselves to reduce conflict, protect civilians, re-establish services, organize elections and rebuild states. This colossal task was also a dangerous one. Armed groups, whether rebels or terrorists, were ready to sabotage the peace process and didn't hesitate to attack civilians or even Blue Helmets. The UN adapted mission mandates as a result. The Blue Helmets could now use force to maintain peace.

In its new policy, the government signalled that it was deploying up to 600 specialized soldiers — what the UN needed most of all — across the globe. The government announced the creation of a $450-million program over three years for peace making and post-conflict stabilization, and planned to fund initiatives aimed at conflict prevention, peace building, capacity building in fragile states, and the protection of the most vulnerable persons during conflicts: women, children and refugees. These ambitious measures were in addition to Canada's compulsory annual contribution of $250 million to UN peacekeeping operations.

Dion reminded his audience that renewing peacekeeping operations wasn't simply a matter of altruism for Canada: "We are returning to peace operations not only because Canadians want to be where the pursuit of peace and protection of civilians requires us to be, but also because it is in Canada's national interest," he said. The destabilization of entire societies such as Mali, the Central African Republic, Darfur, South Sudan, Somalia, Syria and Iraq was a security risk not only for Africa and the Middle East, but also for Europe and, consequently, North America. It was therefore imperative to help solve conflicts by supporting all initiatives along these lines.

While serving as foreign affairs minister, Dion gave 26 major policy speeches, laying out what it meant to pursue a liberal internationalist foreign policy. He developed a guiding principle for the policy — "responsible conviction" — and a method — diplomatic engagement — to make Canada a determined architect of peace. This was, after all, one of his most important goals as minister. He brought together a team of advisers. He had a vision. Now he needed time to implement this policy. Suddenly, the prime minister denied him this opportunity. Trudeau dashed Dion's hopes by firing him.

CHAPTER FIVE
THE MINISTER'S DOWNFALL

During his fourteen months as minister of foreign affairs, Stéphane Dion never met with Prime Minister Trudeau in private to discuss Canada's foreign policy. Not even once. John Baird, who served in the same role in Stephen Harper's government, had a completely different relationship with his boss. He met with the prime minister regularly, even calling him on weekends to discuss particular files. Their conversations were vigorous at times.[1]

In France, meanwhile, Laurent Fabius served almost four years as minister of foreign affairs, under President François Hollande. The two men got together for breakfast every Tuesday at 8:30 sharp for an update on world affairs.[2] It is true that France takes its foreign policy very seriously and has global ambitions.

Dion didn't expect to meet Trudeau as regularly as Fabius met Hollande. Even so, throughout his mandate he periodically requested a meeting with Trudeau to discuss the broad lines of foreign policy in depth. As minister, his job was to articulate Canada's return to the world scene, something Trudeau had campaigned on and had described in detail in the mandate letter he submitted to Dion in November 2015.[3] Dion wanted Trudeau to listen to him, to approve his actions as minister. Strangely enough, Dion never succeeded in landing a one-on-one meeting.

There was always an official reason: scheduling conflicts, packed schedules, foreign travel, poor communications . . .

It is hard to figure out why a one-on-one meeting never took place. One thing is clear, however: Trudeau never showed any particular interest in meeting with his minister. Why? I can offer a possible explanation. But to understand the dynamics, we need to go back in time, analyze the past and the present, and scrutinize the behaviour of the two men.

***

Upon entering political life, Dion came across as straightforward, frank, direct and unaffected. Jean Chrétien's adviser, Eddie Goldenberg, can speak to that. Chrétien asked Goldenberg to meet with Dion and sound him out before Dion was appointed minister. Goldenberg called Dion, inviting him to his house in Ottawa. Dion started their discussion off with a remark that caught Goldenberg completely off guard: "Apparently you are an unreconstructed Trudeauite, a centralist, and completely inflexible."[4] The discussion raged for several hours. After the meeting, Chrétien telephoned his adviser from Asia to ask how the dinner had gone. "Your choice will either be a spectacular success or a spectacular failure, and nothing in between," Goldenberg said. "I cannot predict which it will be."[5]

The prime minister didn't object to Goldenberg's characterization — quite the contrary. He not only liked Dion's style, he went against the rule he had set himself with his ministers, becoming close friends with Dion. An ongoing complicity developed between them. "Before long, I became closer to him than to any other minister. I had always followed Trudeau's example of never showing preference for any one colleague or clique in the Cabinet, because those preferences create jealousies and complications. But Dion proved an exception."[6]

This friendship soon included their respective families, and they continued meeting up on a regular basis. Because Dion liked fishing, Chrétien invited him to the prime minister's official summer residence at Harrington Lake, which was practically unheard of. The two men spent afternoons and evenings together, discussing affairs of state. Chrétien's inner circle was surprised at the close relationship between the two. According to Goldenberg, "They worked together shoulder to shoulder . . . Dion and Chrétien spent a lot of time together in person and on the telephone."[7]

The political and constitutional crisis after the narrow federalist victory in Quebec's October 1995 referendum helps explain why Chrétien got along so well with Dion, the minister responsible for Canadian unity. But there is more to it than that. The prime minister admired Dion's intellectual stature and political courage in facing the Quebec independence movement head on.[8] Had Dion been more reserved and less combative, this friendship would never have gelled.

***

Justin Trudeau and Stéphane Dion didn't develop a close friendship. From the start, it was clear relations between the two were strained. Trudeau did show admiration for Dion in his own memoirs, *Common Ground*. He particularly like Dion's ability to think things through deeply and to address "complex issues."[9] But beyond the sort of flattering comment an active politician is bound to make in his memoirs, Trudeau's frustration with Dion became obvious once Trudeau entered politics.

During the Liberal leadership race in December 2006, Trudeau supported Dion, although this wasn't his first choice. A few weeks later, Outremont MP Jean Lapierre resigned, and Trudeau saw the chance to leap into the political arena. He spoke to the leader about his interest in the Outremont riding, where he lived and where his family had deep roots, but got a frosty reply. Dion made no move to impose Trudeau on the riding organization. "The Outremont riding association vehemently opposed even the rumour of my running there," according to Trudeau. "The leader's office wasn't so keen, either."[10]

Even worse, when Trudeau began checking out the Papineau riding next door to Outremont, "Dion's people indicated to me that Papineau was not right for me either, as they had earmarked it for an 'ethnic' candidate."[11] Trudeau took things in stride, and asked Dion's people what to say if journalists continued asking him to comment on rumours he was going to run in Papineau. "The answer I received was straightforward, and somewhat dismissive: answer journalists' questions however I chose."[12] Undeterred by the ambivalent signals he was getting, Trudeau answered the journalists openly. Yes, he was officially running for the Liberal nomination in Papineau. In public, Dion put on a brave face and congratulated Trudeau for his courage, but behind the scenes "his people were livid."[13] A novice to politics, Trudeau quickly understood that "the leader's office" and the "leader" were one and the same. Despite everything, he won the Liberal nomination in Papineau.

In his memoirs, he took a jab at the Liberal Party and Dion's leadership. "It was for me a tough but illuminating introduction to the internal workings of the Liberal Party of Canada, where infighting, personal agendas, and lack of coherence were the norm."[14]

Trudeau became MP for Papineau in the 2008 general elections, but during his years as part of the Opposition he didn't say a word publicly about his relationship with Dion. He focused instead on learning the ropes as an MP. Sitting on the Opposition benches was hardly the way to raise his profile. And with Dion's resignation as party leader in December that year, Trudeau had to think carefully about his next move. He decided to keep out of the limelight. He wasn't ready to run for the leadership. Michael Ignatieff had an impressive track record as a Harvard professor and world-renowned intellectual. He had run for the leadership in 2006, and ran a second time, replacing Dion as Liberal leader in May 2009. But in the 2011 general election, Ignatieff led the party to its worst defeat at the polls in 140 years. The party was a shambles, and Liberal supporters were seeking a new hope. Trudeau seemed a natural choice. He ran and was elected party leader in 2013.

***

By the time Dion was sworn in as minister in November 2015, Trudeau knew his reputation. Dion wasn't just a fighter and a formidable speaker. He was a man of ideas, with a zeal for detail. He was always arguing. As a minister under Chrétien and Martin, he was always first in the class. Goldenberg writes: "Nobody had better learned the system of Cabinet government [than Dion], no one knew better how to build alliances within the Cabinet, and no minister was more respected by his colleagues."[15]

Dion read everything before turning up for Cabinet meetings — both his own files and those of his colleagues. Goldenberg adds: "No minister was better prepared for Cabinet discussions on a wide variety of issues far beyond national unity, so that when Stéphane Dion spoke, his colleagues put down their coffees, stopped signing correspondence, and listened attentively."[16] He launched into the files of his colleagues, even taking the liberty of correcting them on occasion. This habit of being right and lecturing other people may seem honourable in service of the state, but it riled many of his colleagues. One of Chrétien's former advisers told me some ministers at the time were terrified at the prospect of Dion castigating them during Cabinet meetings. Chrétien had found it all very amusing, since he was surrounded by ministers with strong personalities who could take care of themselves.

But Trudeau didn't appreciate Dion's style. The Cabinet was mostly made up of novices without much political experience. Most of them owed their political existence to Trudeau. With his ministerial experience and intellectual stature, Dion dominated Cabinet. During Cabinet and committee meetings alike, he crossed swords with several ministers, even, rumour had it, reducing some of them to tears.[17] The prime minister found this behaviour annoying. Trudeau doubtless suspected Dion of acting as a second prime minister, taking advantage of Trudeau's own inexperience.

In terms of policy development, Dion found himself in a delicate position. He continually asked the prime minister for a meeting to discuss the broad lines of foreign policy. The party's platform from 2015 and the minister's mandate letter gave some indication of the direction Dion should be taking, but the actual exercise of power meant he needed to set priorities so Canadians and the rest of the world could understand where the country was going on the international scene.

Dion was still getting no answer from Trudeau, so he decided to take matters into his own hands. Starting in March 2016, he began giving a series of speeches explaining how his guiding principle — responsible conviction — and his method — diplomatic engagement — would make Canada a determined architect of peace. This was, after all, one of the key objectives of Canadian diplomacy. Some of his own political advisers and the prime minister's senior adviser for foreign affairs, Roland Paris, were less than enthusiastic about his idea of responsible conviction, and they were uncomfortable with Dion's way of setting foreign policy objectives even before broaching the subject directly with the prime minister.

I was one of those encouraging him to act. He was minister of foreign affairs — he couldn't simply wait in his office for the phone to ring. Dion's first speech on responsible conviction, on March 29, 2016, at the University of Ottawa, got the green light from the Prime Minister's Office, but the next speech, due to be given in May in Quebec City, was not approved in advance. In fact, it sparked a conflict between Dion and Paris.

Dion wanted to take advantage of the St. Laurent Forum on International Security to draw attention to Canada's contribution to this subject. As speechwriter, I first spoke to the policy director, Christopher Berzins, then I presented the minister with a three-page outline, summing up the themes he should cover. Dion then told me to go ahead and write the speech, which highlighted the current hotbeds of insecurity around the world and the steps Canada should take to address them. The structure of the speech followed a classic model. It was couched in the terms of liberal internationalism, an ideology dear to Trudeau's heart. Paris found out about it. The speech was obviously making waves, because Trudeau's foreign affairs adviser was now asking to meet with Dion in person.

On May 3, just days before Dion was due to speak in Quebec City, he and his team met with Paris in the minister's office on Parliament Hill. A storm was brewing as Paris started the discussion. He was concerned that the media would interpret the speech as an overarching statement of the government's foreign policy, whereas, he said, the prime minister had yet to "get his head around" the future direction of Canadian diplomacy. Dion shot back that he had been asking to meet the prime minister for months now, and he meanwhile had to give substance to Canadian diplomacy. He reminded Paris there was nothing out of the ordinary about the speech. The Prime Minister's Office didn't agree.

Paris admitted the meeting with Trudeau ought to have taken place long before, and he would see to setting it up. He suggested Dion stick to listing the Liberal Party's achievements since the election. Dion flatly refused. He wasn't there simply to make watered-down announcements. He wanted to speak about the present and the future. Paris offered the minister an annotated version of the speech, recommending that he take it into consideration. Dion handed me the document so I could incorporate Paris's comments. It was getting late and tempers were short, so I proposed to the others to reread the speech calmly and bring it back for discussion the following day.

Dion worked on a new version overnight. At 6:30 a.m., I got an email from him asking me to phone him. We made the final edits. Dion sent the speech to Paris's office, which proposed two or three small changes. Dion accepted them. The crisis was over. Or was it?

***

A minister is a lightning rod for the prime minister. On tough files, he or she takes it on the chin, defending unpopular government actions, and this was the case for Dion as well. During his fourteen months in office, no foreign affairs minister ever got dragged over the coals so often. Whenever the House of Commons was sitting, he had to answer questions on Canadian strategy against the Islamic State, the fate of Yazidis in Iraq, Canada's re-engagement in the multilateral system, the desirability of keeping the Conservatives' Office of Religious Freedom in operation, relations with Iran, and the crisis in Ukraine. He even had to defend the indefensible, the day Castro died and Trudeau gave a stirring tribute, which led to an outpouring of indignation, including in the United States.

One file in particular came to haunt him on a daily basis: the sale of armoured vehicles to Saudi Arabia. In 2014, the Conservative government approved the sale to the Saudis of vehicles built by General Dynamics Land Systems. The contract was worth an estimated $15 billion over fourteen years and would lead to the creation of more than 3,000 jobs in Canada, mainly in the London, Ontario, region. This sale came at a low point in Canadian–Saudi relations. Raif Badawi, a Saudi blogger, was sent to prison and subjected to public flogging for apostasy and insulting Islam. But his family lived in Canada and regularly kept the public aware of what he was undergoing in Saudi Arabia. Human rights organizations asked Canada to suspend the contract until the blogger was set free.

During the election campaign, the three main parties promised to respect the contract while recalling that the government could block the export licenses if Saudi Arabia contravened export control rules, such as using the vehicles to violate human rights.

The media, mainly in English Canada, came to Badawi's defence and began hammering the government. Journalists threw anything at us they could find. I was one of the first to pay the price. On Easter Monday, March 28, 2016 — usually a quiet day in politics and in the media — *The Globe and Mail* ran a front-page story with the headline "Dion Adviser Critical of Saudi Arms Deal."[18] The journalist based the story on a sentence taken from one of my columns in the Montreal daily *La Presse*, written a few weeks before I started as Dion's adviser. In my column, I wrote that one should not expect Western countries to protest Saudi human rights violations or the war in Yemen too strongly, because "Saudi Arabia has for a long time been buying Western silence by dishing out lucrative civil and military contracts."[19] Dion came to my defence, but the Opposition had a field day.

In April, Dion went ahead with issuing the export licenses, in spite of human rights protests and a court challenge. He trusted Saudi Arabia not to use the vehicle for human rights violations. The Saudi track record on this score was appalling.

Dion struggled with this issue right up to the moment he was fired in January 2017. Some people accused him of doing a lousy job of communicating the government's position. But I find this hard to believe. His replacement as minister, Chrystia Freeland, is still caught between defending human rights versus protecting Canada's economic and geopolitical interests. Trudeau defended the contract during the election campaign, but rarely came to Dion's rescue.

***

In summer 2016, a rumour was doing the rounds in Ottawa's little political world that Dion would soon be on the way out. Some people even said the prime minister planned to name him ambassador to Paris. Obviously, the Prime Minister's Office passed this strategic hint along to a few favoured journalists as a way of sounding out public opinion. Trudeau took a more serious step at the end of August when he took away the role of chair of the ministerial Committee on the environment from Dion and handed it to Heritage minister Mélanie Joly, who posed no threat and was a Cabinet lightweight. Dion was now paying for his clashes with the minister of the Environment, Catherine McKenna, who wanted Canada to follow environmental policies similar to those of the Conservatives. This amounted to an initial reprimand for Dion, who saw it as a public humiliation, considering he had advocated for an ambitious program to address climate change as Paul Martin's minister of the environment.

We advisers began to wonder whether this was the beginning of the end. On October 13, a few of the minister's aides got together for a private dinner at the home of one of his advisers to discuss the situation. Some said Dion was nervous, tired, subject to mood swings. He was totally consumed by work. The minister was interested in everything, and briefing sessions were held at an increasingly frantic pace. Feeling that this hectic rhythm was unproductive, we drew up a plan to keep him focused on four or five major files. A few days later, Dion and his main advisers had dinner in an Ottawa restaurant. He agreed to the list of priorities we presented.

Dion was still waiting for his meeting with Trudeau. He had enjoyed easy access to Jean Chrétien but was now practically forced to take a number and wait outside the Prime Minister's Office. Dion managed to speak to Trudeau briefly on October 29 when the prime minister and his senior ministers headed to Brussels to sign the free trade agreement with Europe. (I wasn't on the trip.) On the plane, Dion raised several subjects, one of which was re-engaging with Russia. Trudeau vacillated, and said there were two distinct views within the government on this subject. According to an eyewitness, the conversation didn't get very far, and Trudeau found Dion's trenchant manner annoying.

In mid-December 2016, a few days before the Christmas holidays, time for a one-on-one meeting suddenly opened up. Unfortunately, Dion's office told Trudeau's office Dion couldn't make it because of a prior commitment — he was going to a funeral. This was a miscommunication. The minister could back out of the commitment. He asked one of his assistants to contact the Prime Minister's Office and arrange a new appointment. Too late. The PMO replied that a meeting would be possible sometime in January.

***

Dion's last days as minister came at the beginning of January 2017. On Thursday, January 5, I returned to the office. Dion was still on holidays and would be back after the weekend. Suddenly, I overheard a conversation. One of the minister's close aides asked his driver to pick Dion up in Montreal on Friday morning and bring him back to Ottawa. The prime minister wanted to see him at 9:00 a.m. This clearly had nothing to do with the one-on-one meeting Dion had been seeking to discuss the broad lines of foreign policy. Something else was happening. I ran into another of Dion's aides and asked how the minister's agenda was shaping up for the following week. He couldn't say yet, but he told me the deputy minister, the number two person at the ministry, had just cancelled a trip to India to stay in Ottawa. It looked like a Cabinet shuffle was coming.

On Friday morning, January 6, Dion went to the Prime Minister's Office. I could only imagine how he felt. For weeks, he had been strung out and anxious, as if he knew in his bones that the end was near. So, this was it. The meeting with Trudeau lasted five minutes. The prime minister handed him his walking papers and offered him a dual post as ambassador in Europe (Germany and the European Union) — a stupid idea dreamed up on the spur of the moment by Trudeau's inner circle. People at Foreign Affairs reacted to the news with sarcasm; the European Union and in Berlin, with indignation.[20] Dion asked why he was being fired. Trudeau said change was needed. Change! Now, that word had a familiar ring to it. In December 2003, Paul Martin replaced Jean Christian as prime minister and began assembling his new Cabinet. At the time, Dion asked if there would be a place for him. Martin, still undecided, said it was unlikely.[21] "But why?" Dion asked Martin at the time. "Because of the need for renewal" came Martin's reply, "the need for renewal is too great."

By way of explanation, Trudeau also mentioned the situation in the United States, with Donald Trump's election as president. Dion said nothing in reply. He left the Prime Minister's Office, sent his driver home and returned to Montreal . . . by bus. I was at the office, feeling uncomfortable since my colleagues still knew nothing about what had just happened. I decided to head to Montreal for the weekend. At the bus station, I saw Dion's director of operations. She was waiting for the minister at the departure door for Montreal. She confirmed he had just been fired. I had hoped to make the trip with him, but he had reached the station ahead of me and was already on his way to Montreal.

The phone rang off the hook all weekend. Calls went back and forth from Dion's home to key personalities and the prime minister. Dion's mentor, Jean Chrétien, was furious. He tried to make Trudeau backtrack, but nothing doing. On Tuesday, January 10, 2017, Trudeau appointed Chrystia Freeland as minister of foreign affairs.

CHAPTER SIX

UNDOING THE CONSERVATIVES' DAMAGE

November 29, 2012, stands as one of the darkest days in the history of Canadian diplomacy. On that day, the UN General Assembly met to discuss a resolution seeking to change Palestine's status at the UN from simple observer to non-member observer state. The meeting was historic. Voting revealed a significant rift among Western countries, isolated Canada, and risked toppling the Australian prime minister.

Palestine had been a UN observer for about thirty years. Several other international organizations had admitted Palestine to full member status. For example, on October 31, 2012, the UNESCO General Assembly welcomed Palestine as its 195th member state. But the resolution tabled at the UN General Assembly didn't go that far. The Security Council was the sole body in a position to authorize the UN General Assembly to vote on admitting a new member. As a permanent member of the Security Council, the United States could veto any such vote. The resolution offered Palestine the prospect of a new international status, enabling it to ratify UN conventions on social or political rights, as well as to endorse treaties open to states and even address complaints to the International Criminal Court.

For some years, the Palestinian leadership had been discussing the prospect of this new status with several other countries. Under the pressure of one country or another, the Palestinian leadership had decided to postpone its application to give the peace process with Israel a better chance of coming to fruition. By 2012, it was clear this process was going nowhere. The Palestinians were exasperated, and so was the rest of the world. Faced with this situation, some UN members tabled a resolution that would grant Palestine a new political status. Debate on the resolution started at 3:00 p.m. The General Assembly was packed to the rafters, and world media were covering the event live.

Mahmoud Abbas, president of the Palestinian Authority, addressed member states, asking them to support the resolution. Then the Israeli ambassador came out against it. The two men gave impassioned speeches, pleading their respective points of view: Here were two visions, based on two foundations of legitimacy, each confronting and ignoring the other. Canadian foreign affairs minister John Baird was in attendance. He had come especially from Ottawa to address the UN General Assembly. He was the only minister of a Western power to come in person. Even his Israeli counterpart was absent.

Baird took his place at the podium and stated: "Canada opposes this draft resolution in the strongest of terms because it undermines the core foundations of a decades-long commitment on the part of the international community and the parties themselves to a two-State solution, arrived at through direct negotiations."[1] Baird added that this position was based on the fact that "Canada has long opposed unilateral actions by either side, as they are unhelpful." Strangely enough, during the four years Baird spent as minister, he never once headed to the General Assembly to denounce unilateral actions taken by Israel. Just when the Palestinians were seeking international recognition, Canada blocked the way, denying them this right. In closing, Baird said Canada would be "considering all available next steps," which was a way of saying it might punish the UN for this "regrettable decision."

Consternation spread through the General Assembly Hall. Here was Canada, a country not willing to lift a finger to support the peace process, but ready to lecture the rest of the world. The European countries, as Palestine's main financial backers, showed their disgust. The president of the General Assembly called for a vote: 138 countries supported the resolution, nine voted against and forty-one abstained. The vote breakdown showed how isolated Canada was. Denmark, Finland, France, Japan, New Zealand and many other Western countries voted for the resolution. Canada voted against, alongside the United States, Israel and a few islands in the South Pacific. Two of Canada's close allies abstained: the United Kingdom and Australia. London explained it wasn't against the resolution, but there were no guarantees from the Palestinians that they wouldn't use their new status to lodge a complaint against Israel before the International Criminal Court.[2] A political crisis broke out in Australia over the Palestinian question. The prime minister, Julia Gillard, was personally opposed to the resolution, but in view of the objections of her Cabinet and MPs, she instructed the delegation to abstain instead.[3]

Baird was furious as he left New York. Back in Ottawa, he recalled Canadian diplomats at the UN, in Israel and in Palestine for consultation. He wanted to review relations with the UN and the Palestinians. Rumour had it he was even considering halting any Canadian assistance for Palestine. In this entire situation, Canada had become so isolated that a sense of discomfort spread throughout Canadian political and media circles. The Toronto conservative daily *The Globe and Mail* called Baird to order. Although the newspaper ran an editorial stating its opposition to the resolution, it saw it as "unreasonable, however, to retaliate against the Palestinians for pursuing their aspirations for statehood, which in themselves are legitimate." The newspaper said the minister "should come down from his high horse and return to the hard, slow work of fostering progress toward a two-state solution."[4]

***

The minister's behaviour towards the UN and its member states showed the low value the Conservatives placed on multilateralism. It also showed the government's deep frustration over having failed to win a non-permanent seat for Canada on the Security Council a year earlier.

It is true the Conservatives had applied for the seat without any particular enthusiasm. They had come to power in 2006 touting a foreign policy agenda that was both nationalist and militarist. They saw the world as split down the middle between good and evil, democracies and dictatorships. This either/or view was like an ideological straitjacket, and it left little room for any other opinions. Harper saw the world as a dark and violent place where the rule of force predominated. According to this view, Canada could count on only a few allies: the United States, Australia, the United Kingdom, three or four European countries and Israel. International organizations were sinister institutions because they were powerless, corrupt and staunchly opposed to Israel. Harper and his ministers did everything they could to cast aspersions on the UN. The prime minister even took perverse pleasure in showing his contempt for the UN. In September 2009, he spent a few hours in New York when the UN General Assembly was in session, but just as President Barack Obama was giving the first speech, Harper left the city to visit a donut factory in Ontario.

If Harper's Canada hated the UN, there was no getting around the fact that the UN was at the heart of the notion of collective security in the world: Peace is built by all, for all. In this respect, the UN Security Council adopted decisions on peace and security that were binding on member states. These decisions provided the framework for the behaviour of states on the international scene, with a view to preventing conflicts. If the decisions failed, then there was a political and legal process to manage or regulate the ensuing conflicts. Even the Americans saw the usefulness of the UN, especially when they needed international backing for some of their own military interventions overseas.

Canada's security partly depended on the proper functioning of the UN and on compliance with its decisions. This explains why Canada made such an enormous investment in the UN since its creation in 1945. Harper was well aware of this long-standing relationship. It was only with reluctance that in 2008 he confirmed the decision of his predecessor, Liberal Paul Martin, to submit Canada's candidacy for a non-permanent seat on the Security Council for 2011–2012.[5]

The prime minister's intervention came late in the process. Actually, voting on the two available non-permanent seats would happen in October 2010. Canada had just two years to rally support among the 191 UN member states.[6] There was a new stumbling block: Canada was competing with Germany and Portugal for one of the two seats reserved for a regional group consisting of Western European and other states. But Germany and Portugal had been campaigning for many years.

Canada was facing a stiff challenge. European countries as a whole, East and West alike (a total of forty-eight), generally voted for European candidates and were good at enlisting the support of other countries. Canada needed to gain the support of most Caribbean, Latin American, African, Asian, Middle Eastern and South Pacific states. Winning a non-permanent seat in the first round of voting took a two-thirds majority (128 votes out of 192).

Many observers noted that Harper's campaign was a catastrophe. The prime minister refused to address the UN General Assembly in 2008 and 2009. Canadian diplomats posted abroad — the very ones the Conservatives distrusted for their "liberal" tendencies — made half-hearted attempts to promote the country's candidacy. In political terms, the Conservatives did everything they could to irritate other countries: They ignored Africa, closely adhered to Israel's position in the conflict with the Palestinians, and annoyed the Europeans and the Americans with their position on climate change.

On September 23, 2010, a few weeks before the vote, Harper finally went to the General Assembly to defend Canada's candidacy. He recalled Canada's commitments to various international engagements: the war in Afghanistan, the rebuilding of Haiti, still reeling from a terrible earthquake several months earlier, and the championing of a maternal, newborn and child health initiative, in which Canada had persuaded other G8 countries to invest several billion dollars. In Harper's mind, there was no doubt Canada deserved a seat on the Security Council. "All these actions are born from Canadian ideals," he told the heads of state and diplomats gathered in the Assembly Hall. "So, allow me to say one thing. This Assembly should know that Canada is eligible to serve on the Security Council. And if we are elected, we will be ready to serve. And if called upon to serve on the Security Council, we shall be informed by these ideals and strive to further them, just as we have striven to implement Security Council resolutions."[7]

The Conservative record was not that bad. It was just that Germany and Portugal had done as well or better on the international scene. On October 10, foreign affairs minister Lawrence Cannon went to the United Nations to take part in voting. He went up and down the aisles of the General Assembly Hall, shaking hands and drumming up support. Since the creation of the UN in 1945, with the notable exception of the vote in 1946, when it lost, Canada had won a non-permanent seat on the Security Council every ten years: in 1948–1949, 1958–1959, 1967–1968, 1977–1978, 1989–1990 and 1999–2000. Each time, Canada had

received an overwhelming majority of votes. Cannon felt confident. Canada had lined up 135 written pledges of support and
about fifteen more verbal pledges.[8] That was enough to win on
the first round.

The president of the General Assembly announced the results.
Germany got 128 votes, the minimum needed to gain a seat. But
wait — Portugal came second with 122 votes, leaving Canada in
third place with 114. The Canadian delegation was in a state of
shock. A new round of voting was needed to fill the second seat.
Canada got seventy-eight votes to Portugal's 113. The message
was clear. The Canadian delegation withdrew its candidacy to
avoid a humiliating third round of voting.

The Conservatives quickly sought to shift the blame for
this defeat, even singling out Liberal leader Michael Ignatieff,
whom they accused of running down Canada's candidacy. But
a more rational explanation soon emerged. UN member states
were unimpressed by Harper's long list of Canadian initiatives
on behalf of the organization. Instead they recalled his harsh
criticism of the UN, his unflinching support for Israel and
his indifference towards Africa. These positions had cost him
the votes of a hundred countries. Even the United States had
refused to campaign for Canada and, according to some sources,
had voted against its candidacy.[9]

An expert on Canadian–US relations at the Hudson Institute
in Washington attributed this defeat to an error made by the
prime minister and his government: The campaign stressed
Canada's past achievements without offering a program of
activity for the future. "What the UN often looks for is a bit
more of a positive case — what it is that you want to be on the
Security Council to do moving forward, so perhaps reforming
peacekeeping or working really hard on the issue of Darfur, or
Afghanistan," the expert told CTV News. "That was really lack-
ing from Canada's bid this year. It was much more of a 'we've

earned it,' rather than a 'here's what we'll do if elected,'" he added.[10]

But in my view, there is a deeper political reason for this defeat. The more countries accede to UN membership, the more they realize the weight of their vote in the General Assembly and the more Canada is competing head-on with other Western candidates. Up to the early 1990s, Canada regularly received massive support on the first round. At the time, Canada's reputation was very strong, thanks to its diplomatic activism on several fronts: the struggle against apartheid in South Africa, the promotion of conventional and nuclear disarmament, Canadian involvement in peacekeeping operations, and the country's substantial foreign aid program.

But at the beginning of the 2000s, another dynamic was set in motion: Canada withdrew from peacekeeping operations and increasingly aligned itself with American and Israeli positions. At the same time, European countries interested in a seat on the Security Council were getting more aggressive on the international scene and more generous towards developing countries that, taken together, represented a hundred states. As soon as three or more Western candidates ran for one or two vacant seats, the voting intentions of member states tended to divide equally between them, which often led to a third and sometimes even a fourth round of voting. The vote in 2010 saw Germany elected on the first round, but only just. Voting turned into a kind of auction between the Western candidates and member states, with the former bidding ever higher to gain a seat. Clearly, Canada wasn't willing to play the game in 2010.[11]

***

The Liberals promised to put Canada back on track. They revered the UN, which Lester B. Pearson had helped found and of which Canada had long been an active partner. Historically, Canada earned its status as a middle power thanks to its commitment to the patient craft of diplomacy alongside other middle powers within international institutions. This activism gave Canada an important voice not only at the UN, but also in peace and security forums, such as disarmament conferences, and allowed it to play a leading role in peacekeeping operations or on mediation missions.

When Trudeau promised to re-engage with the international community, he had to do more than just disagree with the Conservatives. During the meetings of the International Affairs Council, the members reminded him how much the current international situation had changed since the last time Canada had been on the Security Council in 1999–2000.

China had emerged as a superpower; Russia was an aggressive power; the Arab Spring had taken place; Islamist terrorism was virulent; the world was witnessing massive movements of refugees and migrants; climate change and the growing clout of non-state actors were undermining traditional certainties and weakening the international order established just after the Second World War. Besides, technological changes — digital, web-based and social media — were changing the way diplomacy was done, while opening new avenues for economic growth in Western and developing countries. Several members on the Council pointed out that "these changes mean Canada must adapt, renewing the way it engages as actor and partner on the world scene."

One of the Council members said Canada had the means to address this new world configuration: "Canada brings strengths to the world situation, as well as the ability to solve problems, to act as a mediator and protagonist in order to bring change to the world." On this basis, I told the Council, the best way for Canada to make its presence felt internationally was to multiply our strengths by supporting international institutions. One of the key ways to do this was by winning a non-permanent seat on the Security Council. All members of the Council agreed on this point.

But Trudeau added that the first step towards a Security Council seat lay in carefully campaigning other states, "to be more constructive and engaged on the international scene." Council members therefore proposed a major diplomatic offensive in the first 200 days after the election so the Liberal government could consolidate Canada's relations with key partners, while announcing Canada was back on the international scene: brief visits by the prime minister and his main ministers to four continents, a big international event and participation in a major peacekeeping operation two years earlier.

Roland Paris fleshed out the Council's ideas and put them together in an "Open letter to the future prime minister," published a few months before the October 2015 election.[12] "For Canada to succeed — not in the world we have known, but in the world that is emerging — [the prime minister] will need to pursue a forward-looking foreign policy," he wrote. The way to do this required following a key principle of multilateralism: "Canada's interests are served by working constructively with others." This multilateralism, according to Paris, was key to Canada's relationship with the United States, which, in return, gave Canada greater influence over other countries and within international institutions. But, Paris emphasized, multilateral institutions were increasingly under strain because of economic, social, cultural and societal upheaval around the world. This made it all the more important that Canada re-engage in multilateralism and help find solutions to contemporary problems.

He recommended that the future prime minister revive the kind of constructive Canadian diplomacy that had proven so successful before the Conservatives gained power in 2006: "assembling coalitions . . . that produced a ban on anti-personnel mines and established the International Criminal Court," and promoted the concept of the Responsibility to Protect.

The point of this open letter and the Council's advice was to help the new Liberal government undo the damage wrought by the Conservatives and promote Canada's candidacy for a seat on the UN Security Council. But was Trudeau willing to follow this advice?

CHAPTER SEVEN

THE RACE FOR A SEAT ON THE UN SECURITY COUNCIL

On March 16, 2016, a few months after the election, Justin Trudeau headed to UN Headquarters in New York. He told a hall full of enthusiastic UN employees that Canada was back on the global scene. He launched Canada's bid for a non-permanent seat on the Security Council in 2021–2022, committing Canada to a more active role in UN peacekeeping missions. "It's time," the prime minister said. "It is time for Canada to step up once again."[1]

Civil servants at Foreign Affairs in Ottawa knew what a daunting task awaited Canada in its campaign to win a seat on the Security Council. Some of them had been involved in the previous campaign in 2008–2010. This time, a task force was set up to plan and run the campaign. Once a month, this team met in a safe room, far from any microphones or other listening devices. The team included staff at the United Nations and International Organizations Directorate, the assistant deputy minister for Multilateral Affairs, sometimes the Canadian ambassador at the UN as well as his advisers, an adviser to the minister of national defence, and staff from minister of foreign affairs Stéphane Dion's office, among them his chief of staff and me. I served as liaison between the minister's office and different parts of the public service that had an interest in the campaign.

The government built its strategy around a single message: Canada was back on the international scene and was here to help. The prime minister, his ministers, Liberal MPs and all Canadian diplomats abroad had to stick to this message whenever they met the representatives of other states.

Of course, the message was adapted as needed. For example, each time Stéphane Dion met one of his counterparts, Foreign Affairs staff prepared an information sheet summarizing relations between the two countries and the key themes for discussion. The two ministers would review a certain number of questions together — some of them difficult ones — and would commit to finding solutions. Dion would conclude the conversation, asking whether the country his counterpart represented was thinking of supporting Canada's candidacy. He would then transmit the answer to Ottawa, where the task force would add it to a running list consisting of three columns: yes, no, and undecided. Some countries provided written pledges, but most answered verbally. These answers made it possible to adjust strategies and at times to offer an undecided country a faster resolution of a contentious issue in exchange for its vote.

Canada's candidacy met with a favourable response. In March, June and September 2016, I attended several bilateral meetings in Geneva and New York between Dion and around thirty ministers of Foreign Affairs. A good fifteen of them indicated they would vote for Canada, but this meant there were still a lot of negative and undecided responses.

Running for a seat on the Security Council is like an obstacle course. There was no doubt Trudeau was a breath of fresh air on the international scene, but Canada already faced two challenges: It had joined the race late and it needed to demonstrate concretely what its political and diplomatic plans were. The prime minister announced Canada's candidacy in March 2016, and voting would take place in June 2020. At first glance, it might seem Trudeau had four years to line up support in the international community. But in the world of diplomacy, four years is a very short time frame. All the more since the two other countries in the race, Ireland and Norway, had already been campaigning for several years.

The timing was one thing, but political and diplomatic uncertainty was another. Which Canada and which concrete actions did the Trudeau government plan to promote to enlist the support of UN member states for a seat on the Security Council? The Liberal Party's 2015 election platform showcased Canada as "open, accepting and generous," a country of "compassion" towards "those in need."[2] These values underscored programs and policies to welcome refugees, refocus development assistance on helping the poorest and most vulnerable, renew the country's commitment to peacekeeping operations, restore Canada's leading role in the world and invest in Armed Forces. At the same time, the party pledged to promote Canada's economic interests. Re-engaging on the international scene, and especially with the United States, also aimed to boost trade, which would benefit the middle class, a central theme during the Liberal election campaign.

The Liberal Party program said nothing about the most contentious international issues: relations with Russia, the Israeli-Palestinian conflict and the emergence of new powers. It said nothing about future relations with China or even with Africa. But joining the race for a seat on the Security Council meant the government would have to take a clear stand on issues that mattered to UN member states.

Two key issues stood out: the Israeli-Palestinian conflict and the weight of fifty-four African countries in world diplomacy.

***

The Israeli-Palestinian question had preoccupied Canadian diplomacy in the Middle East for seventy years. In 1947, Canada was a member of the United Nations Special Committee on Palestine. The British mandate on Palestine was due to end in May 1948, and the eleven Special Committee members sought a way to replace it. After several months of debate, a majority on the Committee recommended that Palestine be partitioned between an Arab state and a Jewish state, while granting Jerusalem a special international status under the administrative authority of the UN. Pearson played a leading role in favour of partition.[3] From this point onwards, Canada had to navigate between its support for Israel, its relations with the Arab states of the region and the Palestinian question. Canada was quick to condemn the protagonists of different Israeli-Arab wars (in 1948, 1956, 1967 and 1973) and took part in all UN peacekeeping missions in the region. Canadian officers commanded several of these missions, among them the one created in 1956 by Pearson following the Suez Crisis (the United Nations Emergency Force), which earned him the Nobel Peace Prize the following year.

The Israeli-Palestinian conflict is a minefield for any country seeking a solution there. It is a conflict charged with such powerful symbols and emotions that even the most powerful person on the planet, the president of the United States, was barely able to take any decisive action there. In January 2017, shortly after gaining power, Donald Trump promised to move the American embassy from Tel Aviv to Jerusalem, which was not recognized internationally as the Israeli capital. The status of Jerusalem lies at the heart of the Israeli-Palestinian conflict. Trump's announcement unleashed a storm of protest, and he had to backtrack. But, on November 6, he announced that the United States was recognizing Jerusalem as capital of Israel, while postponing the move of the US embassy there, and in May 2018 he moved the US embassy there.

Forty years earlier, a Canadian politician had found himself in the same predicament. A few days after taking office in June 1979, Conservative Prime Minister Joe Clark announced that the Canadian embassy was moving from Tel Aviv to Jerusalem, in fulfilment of a promise made to the Jewish community during the election campaign. The decision caused such an outcry, Clark had to name a former Conservative leader to study the issue in depth and come back with a report. The report, which came out the following October, recommended that Canada not undertake to move the embassy. Clark acquiesced: The Canadian embassy would stay in Tel Aviv.

Once the United Nations developed the partition plan for Palestine, Canada remained a "fair" and "impartial" actor in the Israeli-Palestinian conflict, at least up to the middle of the first decade of the twenty-first century. According to one Canadian observer, Canada's support for Israel and for Palestinian aspirations "were not seen as mutually exclusive but rather as mutually reinforcing, as Israel security, in this vision, would be reinforced and consolidated through the creation of a viable Palestinian state."[4]

At the same time, Canadian foreign policy began siding with Israel under the Mulroney government, from 1984 to 1993. The Conservative prime minister made no secret of his abiding friendship for Israel, even paying tribute to Israel as "a better ally, a great ally" as one of "Canada's four traditional allies": the United States, the United Kingdom, France and Israel.[5] This was the first time the Jewish state was added to the list of Canada's three historical allies. Once Mulroney named Clark foreign affairs minister, he let Clark serve as the pro-Arab member of Cabinet. This was a way of protecting Canada's economic interests in the Arab world. Even so, Mulroney wasn't willing to interact directly with Yasser Arafat, the leader of the Palestinian Authority, whom he considered a "terrorist."[6]

Mulroney was resolutely pro-Israeli: he was concerned about the frightening rise of anti-Semitism virtually everywhere in the world, particularly in the West. This new anti-Semitism was different from the 1930s version: It now took the guise of anti-Zionism, questioning the very existence of the Jewish state. Mulroney's position was all the more solid as the UN General meeting had adopted a resolution in 1975 determining that Zionism was a form of racism and racial discrimination. The UN revoked the resolution in 1991.

On entering office in October 1993, Jean Chrétien's Liberals opened a new chapter in relations between Canada and the Middle East. A month earlier, Israel and the Palestine Liberation Organization had signed the Oslo Accord at the White House, signalling a significantly new relationship. It was a time of excitement. Peace finally seemed within reach. Canada was ready to support the peace process and had already chaired a multilateral group on Palestinian refugees.

Jean Chrétien avoided taking an ideological stance. He preferred emphasizing concrete and pragmatic actions liable to bring Israel and Palestine closer together. In 2000, he travelled for twelve days in the region, the longest visit to the Middle East ever made by a Canadian prime minister.[7] But as things turned out, Canada had limited influence on the Israeli-Palestinian question. The United States completely dominated the situation, leaving Europe and Canada minimal room for any initiatives.

Chrétien's departure from office and Paul Martin's years as Liberal prime minister (2003–2006) saw Canada moving towards an increasingly pro-Israeli position, a move that was accentuated under the Conservative Stephen Harper (2006–2015). This change had diplomatic ramifications, particularly at the UN. Every autumn, the UN General Assembly discussed around twenty resolutions concerning the Israeli-Palestinian conflict, in addition to Israeli-Arab concerns, then voted on them. Each time the resolutions singled out Israel, which was roundly condemned. The cumulative effect of these votes was to stigmatize a particular UN member, whereas other countries in the region were shielded from criticism although they bore responsibility for ongoing conflicts. In the absence of resolutions targeting other Middle Eastern states, the Harper government stopped supporting the resolutions singling out Israel.

This position might seem to indicate Canada was breaking with the UN. But the situation was more complex than that. In 2016, Steven Seligman of Dalhousie University in Halifax published a study measuring this perception and Canada's increasingly pro-Israeli stance under the Chrétien, Martin and Harper governments, as shown by voting at the UN General Assembly between 1994 and 2015.[8] Seligman analyzed 888 votes by Canada on fifty recurring resolutions over the twenty-one-year period, such as the American embargo against Cuba, nuclear weapons and the Israeli-Palestinian conflict. "Canada's voting record on most issues did not change after the Conservatives came to power in 2006," he writes.[9] "The one important exception, however, was the Israeli-Palestinian conflict, in which the Harper government moved Canada's position to more closely align with Israel and the United States."[10]

There were many resolutions on a range of contentious issues. Some addressed the Israeli occupation of the Golan Heights, which is Syrian territory, while others addressed Palestinian refugees, the right of Palestinians to self-determination, the status of Jerusalem, Israeli settlements in the occupied territories or the risk of nuclear proliferation in the Middle East. While these resolutions were justified under international law, the wording of the resolutions is often polemical and aggressive. Even so, the Chrétien government voted in favour of most of them. It abstained on four resolutions. "In each case, Canada's vote aligned with the United Kingdom and France, and very nearly aligned with Australia, but diverged from the United States and Israel."[11]

Under Martin, Canada began moving closer to Israel. Whereas the Chrétien government had abstained on four resolutions, the Martin government started voting against. Once the Harper government entered office, Canada's position became more radical. Between 2006 and 2010, Canada switched its "yes" votes for abstentions and its abstentions for "no" votes. In 2011, "during the majority years of the Harper government, Canada voted against eighteen of the twenty-one resolutions addressing the Middle East, while abstaining on two more."[12] Seligman's analysis reveals that Canada had now moved away from the United Kingdom and France to join the American-Israeli camp.

The Harper government paid the price for abandoning principle and taking consistently pro-Israeli positions in international forums while politicizing its voting on UN resolutions. This partly accounts for Canada's failure to win a seat on the Security Council in 2010 as well as the poor relations it had with European allies and the Arab world on Middle Eastern issues.

*****

Did Justin Trudeau want to strike a more balanced position on the Israeli-Palestinian conflict, breaking with the Conservative legacy of Canada's diplomatic isolation? He gave this impression before his October 2015 election win. The Liberal leader rarely mentioned the Israeli-Palestinian conflict, and even when he did, it was only to repeat his diplomatic adviser's well-worn line: "We should uphold Israel's right to exist and its security, but without diminishing the rights of Palestinians."[13]

During the leadership debate on foreign policy on September 28, 2015, Trudeau recalled the Canadian political consensus on the question, accusing Harper of making Israel "a domestic political football," whereas "all three of us" federal leaders — NDP leader Thomas Mulcair was also part of the debate — "support Israel as any Canadian government will."

But Trudeau and Harper didn't see eye to eye ideologically. As incoming prime minister, Trudeau was first and foremost a pragmatic leader who was constantly seeking consensus and compromise, on the Israeli-Palestinian conflict as much as on other issues of domestic or foreign policy. He didn't share Harper's Manichean worldview, pitting the forces of good against the forces of evil. For his part, Harper took pleasure in highlighting and exaggerating any antagonism, any differences, as a way of defining his own position and forcing his adversaries to choose their camp.

On Israel, Harper crafted an apocalyptic account of a country under siege by the forces of evil and whose defence was imperative for democracies and especially for Canada. According to this account, "Canada is the most pro-Israeli country in the world," writes Jeffrey Simpson, a renowned columnist for *The Globe and Mail*. But "this statement is completely wrong. The Harper government may be the most pro-Israeli government in the world, but the population is not."[14] Opinion polls confirm Simpson's analysis.[15]

How would Trudeau react, as incoming prime minister, to the recurring resolutions on the Israeli-Palestinian conflict at the UN General Assembly? The Liberal government entered office at the beginning of November 2015, and Trudeau supported Harper's previous positions. At Foreign Affairs, however, the incoming minister, Stéphane Dion, told his civil servants to review the whole Israeli-Palestinian question. He asked for an analysis of each of the resolutions and wanted to see what options Canada had that respected the principles of international law without stigmatizing Israel.

In the minister's office, this was such a sensitive file that every-
body got involved. The chief of staff, the policy director, the
communications director, the legislative affairs director and I set
to work. We consulted several Jewish community leaders and the
Israeli embassy. For the government, voting on these UN resolutions was a high-stakes matter. The government had to take into
consideration the likely response and behaviour of Jewish and
pro-Israel voters, the views of Jewish MPs and Canada's relations
with Israel. The government knew Jewish voters had split up into
pro-Harper and pro-Trudeau camps in 2015, and loyalty towards
Israel was a key test defining each of the camps as they sparred
with one other.[16]

Pro-Israel groups exert significant influence in Canada. In
2016, according to the Lobbying Commissioner, the Centre for
Israel and Jewish Affairs ranked fifth among the twenty most
active organizations and companies seeking to meet with governmental decision makers.[17]

Civil servants at Foreign Affairs worked for several months
on the recurring UN resolutions file. Finally, on September 13,
a few days before the opening of the UN General Assembly,
the civil servants met with Dion and his advisers. The minister
started the meeting by recalling three key points: Canada should
denounce the way Israel was being stigmatized at the UN; Canada
should take a constructive approach to the resolutions; and finally,
Canada should vote on each resolution taking into account the
principles of international law. The civil servants promised to
respond quickly. They came back a few weeks later with several
different options, one of which included changing Canada's votes
on a few resolutions while striking a balance between Dion's three
key points.

Dion forwarded the option chosen to the prime minister.
Trudeau vacillated. One day, he agreed to change Canada's voting
on a few resolutions; the next day, he disagreed with the idea.

Dion pointed out that the option chosen enshrined the principles Canada defended on the international scene while demonstrating Canadian solidarity with Israel. A few days later, while Dion and I were visiting Kenya on government business, some of Trudeau's close advisers reminded him of the promise made to the Jewish community during the election campaign not to change Canada's voting at the UN. The prime minister backtracked.[18] Six months spent looking for the most balanced option for Canada came to nothing.

***

Africa was another key factor to consider in running for a seat on the Security Council. On this score, 2016 started off well. Dion and I visited Nigeria, Kenya and Ethiopia. During that year, the prime minister also made a brief stop in Liberia, then spent two days at the Francophonie Summit in Madagascar. In addition, the International Development minister and the Defence minister visited several other African countries. This was the first time in twelve years that so many Canadian ministers had travelled to Africa. The Conservatives had preferred to ignore Africa and reduced foreign aid there, while launching the maternal, newborn and child health initiative, which benefited many African countries. The Conservatives had preferred highlighting relations with Latin America which, it was true, represented a rapidly growing commercial market. This strategy was justifiable. But the Conservatives made the mistake of underestimating the diplomatic and economic potential of Africa.

They ignored Africa at their peril. Comprising fifty-four states, the African continent is the largest political block on the planet. These states are all UN members and often voted together on items on the UN agenda. In economic terms, analysts considered Africa to be the next frontier. In 2013, *The Economist* published a very positive supplement on Africa with a catchy title: "A Hopeful Continent." The weekly news magazine based its analysis on statistics and official reports: Some African countries had annual growth rates approaching 10 per cent, while the average for the continent was 5 per cent; about 100 million Africans earned more than $3,000 a year and constituted the core of an emerging middle class; trade with the rest of the world was growing rapidly; conflicts were diminishing; and mobile telephone use was exploding, with the number of phone owners even surpassing that of several European countries. According to the World Bank, "Africa could be on the brink of an economic take-off, much like China was 30 years ago and India 20 years ago."

Both the great powers and the emerging powers were taking advantage of this situation. France maintained the strongest presence in Africa of any foreign country in every category — its military presence there was unrivalled — but China had a strong diplomatic, economic and even cultural impact there. With fifty embassies and forty-five Confucius Institutes in Africa's fifty-four countries, China had just opened its first military base abroad, in Djibouti, and deployed altogether about 2,000 Blue Helmets in UN peacekeeping operations on the continent. In 2009, China became Africa's leading trade partner and hoped to double trade by 2020, reaching $400 billion a year. China's investments in Africa ranked fourth, behind France, the United States and the United Kingdom. A million Chinese people were stationed in Africa as labourers, industrialists, doctors and humanitarian workers. Between 2007 and 2013, the Chinese president, prime minister and foreign affairs minister returned to Africa repeatedly, visiting twenty-eight countries there.

Turkey, Brazil, India, Japan, Germany and even South Korea were expanding their presence there. Most of these countries followed the French model in pursuing political relations with African states: They organized summits, sometimes yearly, with all African leaders, providing opportunities for the leaders to get to know one another better and securing advantages on diplomatic and economic fronts.

Canada had until recently been a country that mattered in Africa. Canada had significant assets on that continent: It had no history of colonial exploitation there; its two official languages — French and English — were the two most widely spoken on the continent; its missionaries and teachers worked in schools and universities that educated local elites; its humanitarian and volunteer workers were devoted heart and soul to programs that were widely appreciated; Canadian industrialists were present in the mining industry.

In 2005, at the high point of Canada's presence in Africa, the country had twenty-six embassies on the continent. Canada focused part of its foreign aid on fourteen countries. It took part in peacekeeping operations, for example in the Congo, the Central African Republic, Ethiopia and Eritrea. Several major Canadian diplomatic initiatives — the Ottawa Treaty banning anti-personnel mines, the creation of the International Criminal Court, the concept of the Responsibility to Protect, which we discussed in previous chapters — were well received in most African countries. Canada's voice was heard throughout Africa. In 1998, Canada easily obtained a non-permanent seat on the UN Security Council during the first round of voting, garnering no fewer than 131 votes out of 191.

Pierre Trudeau and Brian Mulroney had both shown particular interest in Africa, but it was really under Jean Chrétien that Africa was made a priority for government action. This helps explain how Canada secured a seat on the Security Council. In his memoirs, Chrétien admits that his interest in Africa arose from necessity. "Quite quickly and unexpectedly, however, I became absorbed in the issues of Africa, not least because all but a few of the African nations are members of either the Commonwealth or

La Francophonie. The more I met with their leaders, the more involved I became in their agendas, the more I wanted Canada to help."[19]

Starting in 1994, he urged his G7 counterparts to put Africa on the summit agenda. In 2001, G7 leaders called on Chrétien to develop an action plan for Africa. The following year, in Kananaskis, Alberta, he presented the New Partnership for Africa's Development. The government, meanwhile, created a special $500-million fund to finance aid projects and investments on the continent.

The Conservative victory in 2006 changed Canada's priorities. The government closed embassies, reduced foreign aid, cut back on ministerial visits on the continent and antagonized Africans through its position on the Palestinian question. It hardly came as a surprise in 2010 when an overwhelming majority of African countries voted against Canada's candidacy for a seat on the UN Security Council.

***

Would Africa become a priority for Justin Trudeau's incoming Liberal government? Trudeau was no stranger to Africa. At the age of twenty-three, he had visited a half-dozen Western African countries, but he didn't say much about them in his memoirs, *Common Ground*. It was only once Trudeau became Liberal leader that he began showing an interest on the subject, for example during the meetings of the International Affairs Council.

The members of the Council addressed two main themes with respect to Africa: peacekeeping operations and development assistance. In summer 2014, African conflicts made the headlines on a regular basis, leading to vigorous debate. The situations in the Central African Republic and South Sudan were particularly discouraging. I reminded my colleagues on the Council that

Canada had taken part in the UN mission in the Central African Republic in 1998, and we knew this was a francophone country. Why not go back there? We soon agreed as a Council to propose returning there as a priority for the next Liberal government.

At its December 2014 session, the Council invited three experts to address us on development assistance. Our discussions focused on two questions: Does this assistance produce results? What are the next steps? According to these experts, assistance produced results even if, in some situations, it might not actually work. Moreover, they drew diverging conclusions about the results of such aid. But one thing was clear: Development assistance required a long-term commitment and you should never hope for immediate results.

These three experts drew the Council's attention to one major trend: Assistance was increasingly oriented towards the economic interests of Canadian companies, especially in the mining sector. They felt it was time to review the Canadian model of foreign aid and reach out to the poorest and most vulnerable, particularly girls and women. The experts called on a future Trudeau government to increase development assistance once it took office. One of the attendees at the meeting even proposed that the Liberals recommit to the goal Pearson had set forty years earlier of dedicating 0.7 per cent of the gross national income to foreign aid, a goal met by the United Kingdom, Denmark, Norway, Sweden and the Netherlands.

Trudeau didn't respond to this proposal. The Liberal election platform incorporated some of the Council's ideas — focusing on the most vulnerable and poorest countries, reviewing current policies — but was careful not to make specific financial commitments to such initiatives. The following year, however, the Liberal Party promised during the election campaign to do more. "A Liberal prime minister, Lester B. Pearson, led the UN commission that recommended the ODA's 0.7 per cent of GNI goal, and a Liberal

government under Justin Trudeau will aspire to reach this alloca-
tion."[20] Two years later, Trudeau broke that promise.

On June 7, 2017, Trudeau announced a new feminist foreign
policy after the government had undertaken a complete review
of foreign aid policies following broad national and international consultations with associations. Throughout the election
campaign, Trudeau presented himself as a feminist. He promised
a government with equal numbers of male and female ministers,
as well as programs promoting gender equality. The goal of
feminist foreign aid was to "amplify the voices of women and
girls and support their opportunities to choose their own future
and fully contribute to their community."[21] Making a priority of
women and girls fulfilled the campaign promise of coming to the
assistance of the poorest and most vulnerable.

This new feminist policy direction was laudable, but the
underlying trend of official development assistance (ODA)
provided by Canada was disturbing: ODA had been in grad-
ual decline for forty years. In 1978, the ODA had accounted
for 0.54 per cent of GNI — its best year since the launch of
development assistance in the 1960s.[22] At that time, Canada
seemed within reach of the goal set by Pearson: 0.7 per cent of
GNI. Faced with the Canadian economic situation and a series
of government deficits, the Chrétien and Martin governments
cut ODA to 0.23 per cent of GNI in 2003. Harper brought it
back up to 0.32 per cent, but Justin Trudeau cut ODA to 0.27
per cent.[23]

This performance put Canada in fifteenth place among
the twenty-nine members of the Organisation for Economic
Co-operation and Development's Development Assistance
Committee. And the worst was yet to come. The federal budget
of 2017 provided for no increase in ODA over the next five
years. According to the Canadian Council for International
Cooperation, this meant Canada's ODA would actually decline in

real terms: "[B]y the end of this government's first mandate it will have the lowest average commitment to ODA as a percentage of GNI in half a century."[24] Meanwhile, in June 2017, the government announced a 74 per cent increase in military spending over the next decade.

***

Africa was key to Canada's return to the international scene, and Africa would in good measure account for Canada's success or failure in winning a seat on the Security Council in 2021–2022. I let Stéphane Dion know I was planning a re-engagement strategy for Canada on the African continent. In December 2016, the sixteen-page document was ready. I recommended that the government pursue a three-pronged strategy on the diplomatic, economic and security fronts. Otherwise, we were headed for failure.

Diplomatic action was the first component of this re-engagement strategy. It required a physical presence on the ground and sustained relations with African leaders. For a dozen years now, Canada's diplomatic impact in Africa had been waning. We had gone from twenty-six to twenty-one embassies and missions on a continent with fifty-four countries. Budgets were cut; diplomatic offices were tiny. And yet a number of foreign powers were bulking up their diplomatic presence. Turkey now had forty embassies in Africa, South Korea had twenty-two and Norway — a country of five million inhabitants, now competing with Canada for a seat on the Security Council in 2020–2021 — had twenty-one. Needless to say, opening a mission was a costly venture, but it didn't necessarily require buying property. There were precedents for sharing office space. In Mali, the Canadian diplomatic office has for a long time housed the British diplomatic mission. In Cambodia, the British mission was home to Canadian diplomats.

Canadian politicians needed to reach out to Africans if they wanted Canada to be taken seriously. The prime minister and his ministers needed to make more frequent visits there. But in 2016, Justin Trudeau turned down an invitation to speak at the summit of heads of state of the African Union in Kigali, Rwanda. He wasn't invited the next year. He spent a few hours in Liberia and then two days in Madagascar for the Francophonie Summit. Some of his ministers travelled more regularly to Africa — particularly the foreign affairs, defence and international affairs ministers — but this wasn't enough to make the difference.

Other powers kept very busy in Africa, some of them imitating the French example of Franco-African summits. China, India, Japan and the United States regularly organized this kind of summit: The leader of the host country took the time to meet every African leader in attendance one on one. Even Israel played the summit card, meeting with its African partners to discuss investments and security, but also the candidacy of the Jewish state for a seat on the Security Council in 2019–2020. Israel understood perfectly that in this subtle diplomatic game, every vote counted. Canada couldn't just sit on the sidelines. It had to be ambitious and organize a summit of its own.

The second component of this re-engagement strategy was bolstering Canada's economic presence in Africa. In moving unilaterally to revamp the North American Free Trade Agreement, US president Donald Trump had shown only too clearly how dependent Canada was on the United States, and how little room to manoeuvre Canada had on the global scene. Canada had long grown used to its comfortable relationship with its southern neighbours and hadn't tried hard enough to diversify its economic relations with the rest of the world.

In his day, Pierre Trudeau had tried increasing trade with Asia and Europe, but his overtures had failed. Justin Trudeau seemed to grasp the strategic importance of diversifying Canada's trading partners. A few months before the October 2015 election, he sounded the alarm. In a speech on Canada–US relations, Trudeau said the time had come for Canada "to strengthen our ties with burgeoning global markets in Asia and Africa, in particular."[25]

Now was the time to act. Canada's economic presence in Africa was mostly restricted to the mining, oil and gas sectors. Canadian companies were present in forty-three of the continent's fifty-four countries. But the 2017 report of the African Development Bank on the continent's economic prospects indicated that growth in Africa was less based on natural resources than it had been in the past: Growth was now increasingly related to improving the business environment and macroeconomic governance. The diversification of the African economy and the growth of its middle class required massive investments in several sectors: infrastructure, information and communication technologies, energy, food processing, transport and hotels. It was striking how absent Canada was from all of these sectors.

The third and final component of this re-engagement strategy was security. If Canada wanted to benefit from economic growth in Africa and expand its own influence on the international scene, it was in Canada's interest to contribute to conflict resolution there. Africa had the largest number of conflicts and crises in the world. Eight of the UN's fifteen peacekeeping missions were stationed there, as well as seven European Union military and civilian peacekeeping missions, and an African Union mission.

In 1996, the outbreak of war in the eastern part of the Democratic Republic of the Congo was referred to as "Africa's first world war." Since that time, one African country in two experienced war, terrorist activities or violent political strife. The regions most affected were the Sahel Belt of Africa, stretching from Senegal to Somalia, and parts of tropical West and Central Africa. Conflicts and terrorist attacks destabilized already fragile African states, sending hundreds of thousands of migrants into exile, across the Sahara to the Mediterranean, then overseas to Europe. The African Union couldn't stabilize the continent on its own. Canadians were now direct victims of these conflicts: Nine Canadians have been killed in terrorist attacks in Ouagadougou, Burkina Faso, since 2016.

Canada's very limited involvement in UN peacekeeping missions and counter-terrorism missions in Africa fly in the face of Canada's national interests.[26] Insecurity in Africa can only have a negative effect on the security of Europe and North America. And it seems extremely odd that in African countries where Canadian mining companies are most active — Mali, Niger and the Democratic Republic of the Congo — it is Chinese Blue Helmets and French and American anti-terror forces that are actually hard at work stabilizing these countries.

***

The annual session of the UN General Assembly provides a useful channel of communication for the interaction of states. Once the session is opened in mid-September, heads of state and of government from the entire world converge on New York to make their voices heard in the community of nations. It's also a special moment for meetings between leaders who don't get to see each other regularly. Trudeau went to the General Assembly in 2016 and 2017, addressing his peers there. In 2018, he went to the UN but didn't address the General Assembly.

Addressing the UN General Assembly is a daunting exercise. Each speaker is expected to provide concrete and practical answers to the great international questions of the hour and to show that his or her country is worthy of a seat on the Security Council. The prime minister missed his opportunity twice. In 2016, he started his address by telling the delegates what it was like meeting with Canadians during the election campaign the previous year. He devoted a major part of the speech to himself and his efforts to improve the employment outlook for the Canadian middle class. He said nothing about major international issues, other than the fact Canada was looking to attract members of the middle class — doctors, lawyers, teachers — in Syrian refugee camps.

In 2017, Trudeau told delegates at the General Assembly how his government was working to restore Indigenous peoples' place within Canadian society. This issue is important, because international organizations are increasingly concerned about the fate of minorities and Indigenous populations, such as the Yazidi minority in Iraq or the Rohingya minority in Myanmar. The Canadian experience in reconciliation could prove interesting for the rest of the world. But Trudeau said nothing about Canada's position on issues that rocked the foundations of the world order and were on everyone's mind in the Assembly Hall: Syria, terrorism, the war against poverty, the environment, migration, Iranian and North Korean nuclear technology. Just a few hours earlier, the French president, Emmanuel Macron, and the British prime minister, Theresa May, among others, tackled these issues head on, positioning their respective countries as key players in global governance.

Of course, nobody expected Canada to solve the North Korean crisis or disagreements about Iran's nuclear program within a day or two, or single-handedly to negotiate an agreement on Iran's nuclear program. But member states — that is, countries poised to vote — expected a country running for a seat on the Security Council to say in concrete terms why it deserved to be elected. Yet Trudeau provided nothing tangible to induce other countries to support Canada's candidacy.

***

To this day, Canada's re-engagement with Africa remains modest, and the Trudeau government continues to support the positions of the Harper government on the Israeli-Palestinian conflict. And yet it was precisely on these grounds that Canada's candidacy for a seat on the Security Council failed in 2010. If Trudeau's approach doesn't change, Canadians may be in for a rude awakening in June 2020 when General Assembly members decide which two of the three candidates — Canada, Norway and Ireland — deserve a seat on the Security Council.

CHAPTER EIGHT

THE DIFFICULT RETURN OF CANADA'S BLUE HELMETS

Angelina Jolie slowly made her way to the podium in Vancouver, where a hundred defence ministers from around the world had gathered for the traditional group photo. She was the special guest at the November 15, 2017, ministerial conference devoted to UN peacekeeping. All eyes were on her. As an actress, model, philanthropist and goodwill ambassador, Jolie had long been defending humanitarian causes and was particularly interested in the protection of animals and the environment. She had also experienced personal adversity: She chose to have preventive mastectomies to reduce her high risk of breast cancer.

The actress was an icon, and Justin Trudeau loves icons, especially when he can use them to dazzle an audience, steering attention away from the fact that he was unveiling weak government policy.

Jolie gave a speech on sexual violence towards women and girls in war zones. She accused the states represented inn Vancouver of not doing enough to stop it. Jolie was right. Sexual violence was on the rise and was damaging the reputation of the Blue Helmets, even if they weren't the only ones responsible. The UN had sought to address this complex problem for two decades, but implementing solutions was proving difficult.

The Vancouver ministerial conference was not just focused on sexual violence: It was intended to serve as a venue for announcements about major new government commitments to UN peacekeeping operations. And with Canada hosting the meeting, the audience anxiously awaited Prime Minister Trudeau's keynote speech, especially since he had already made Canada's return to the international scene and its renewed commitment to peacekeeping part of his election platform in 2015. Starting in August 2016, the Trudeau government unveiled an ambitious policy on peace operations, which was met with enthusiasm at the UN. This policy broke with the former Conservative government, which had shown the greatest contempt for peacekeeping and the Blue Helmets during its nine years in power.

Now was the time for the Prime Minister to deliver. But the speech he gave was long and meandering, more form than substance, and the gathered ministers could see Canada was now retreating from the position it had taken in 2016. It would make only an extremely modest contribution. There would be no immediate military or police deployment, nor would much-needed equipment be provided for peace operations. Canada would not announce until March 19, 2018, that it was sending a contingent to Mali. This contribution fell well short of the ambitious policy announced in 2016. (I will return to this subject below.) So, what was really happening? To answer this question, we need to go back in time and recall how Canada, the country that created the Blue Helmets thanks to Lester B. Pearson, had become a minor player by the time Justin Trudeau came to power.

***

Canada had made its involvement in UN peacekeeping one of the pillars of its foreign and defence policy for many decades. Peacekeeping even got swept up into Canadian national identity, at home and abroad: Here was a nation of peacekeepers.[1] Up till the middle of the 1990s, Canada took part in all UN peacekeeping operations.

For half a century, politicians, historians, researchers and even business people regularly maintained that peacekeeping was part of Canadians' DNA. And the whole planet believed this to be case, even to the point of absurdity. The famous American political scientist Francis Fukuyama claimed in a book on military interventions and nation-building after conflicts that some military contingents were incapable of going from peacekeeping to peace enforcement because "some contemporary armies, such as Canada's, have trained specifically for peacekeeping missions, whereas others, such as the US military, train for classical war-fighting."[2]

This statement is clearly wrong as far as Canada is concerned. The Canadian military train for warfare. But Fukuyama can be excused for this mistake. Canadian foreign and defence policy actually played up the country's role in peacekeeping until the Conservatives took power in 2006, and this could well have influenced his judgment. After all, the Chrétien government's 1994 white paper on defence said: "We uphold a proud heritage of service abroad. We take pride in Lester B. Pearson's Nobel Prize for Peace."[3]

The Canadian government, diplomats and politicians reinforced the same message. The Canadian people internalized the message to the point that Molson, the brewing giant, used it in advertising. In 2000, an ad on English-language TV showed a young man ranting: "I believe in peacekeeping, not policing. My name is Joe and I am Canadian."

Strangely enough, just when Joe Canadian was touting peacekeeping as part of national identity, Canada was moving towards more robust interventions bordering on peace enforcement. The first half of the 1990s was a particularly traumatic period for UN peacekeeping operations in general and above all for Canadians serving in them. The failures of the Blue Helmets in Somalia, Bosnia and Rwanda shook the conscience of the world and affected Canadians directly. For the first time, Canadian military had stood as powerless witnesses of extreme acts of violence. Two generals — Lewis MacKenzie and especially Roméo Dallaire — had first-hand experience of UN shortcomings and large-scale massacres on a daily basis.

These experiences led the Canadian and other Western governments to redefine the nature of modern conflict. Traditional peacekeeping no longer seemed capable of addressing situations of internal strife, civil wars and ethnic cleansing that increasingly faced the UN.

The Chrétien government assessed post–Cold War era changes. In its White Paper of 1994, the Liberal government said Canada needed to raise the ceiling of 2,000 servicemen and women abroad set by previous governments. It promised to increase the number of troops earmarked for UN operations to 4,000, and even to deploy up to 10,000, if necessary. The bar was now so high there was no way to reach it. Starting in 1996, while millions of Rwandan refugees poured into the forests of the eastern part of the Democratic Republic of the Congo, Chrétien tried to mount a rescue mission; it was a disaster, because Canada's ambitions exceeded its resources. The mission was dropped because Canada lacked the operational ability to see it through.[4]

Meanwhile, Lloyd Axworthy became foreign affairs minister and drafted a humanitarian and interventionist program focusing on human security and human rights. Canada called on UN member states to respond strongly to human rights violations. This campaign led to the creation of the International Criminal Court in 1998 and the formulation of the concept of the Responsibility to Protect in 2001. At the same time, Canada gradually withdrew from UN peacekeeping operations, committing instead to more robust NATO operations in Bosnia, Kosovo and especially Afghanistan, or coalitions of the willing during multi-national interventions in East Timor and Haiti. The number of Canadian military and police taking part in UN missions dropped from 2,700 in 1994 to about sixty in December 2017.

Several factors explain this change. On the international level, conflict situations in the post–Cold War era are said to be charac-terized by civil wars and massacres. Peacekeepers therefore need to engage more aggressively, which the UN is not allowed to do for political and material reasons. As a result, NATO and regional organizations have offered their support, only too happy to define new roles for themselves after the fall of the Berlin Wall.

NATO's engagement, for example, offers three advantages to Western countries: First, the organization is more homogen-eous than the UN, and its members have worked together since 1949; second, NATO can deploy considerable military power in fulfilling a robust mandate; and third, NATO's engagement guarantees that the United States will take part in the interven-tion. The UN relied on NATO to undertake more robust peace mandates in Bosnia, Kosovo and Afghanistan. A division of labour settles in at the UN between those preferring traditional UN peacekeeping, and those favouring more violent missions.

Finally, the growing number of peacekeeping operations led to a quantitative and qualitative increase among country contribu-tors, particularly from Southern ones. In 1982, seven of the top ten contributors to UN peacekeeping operations were Western. By 1994, six of the top ten were Southern countries.[5] This trend continued over the next few years, with NATO and the EU opting to set up their own peacekeeping operations, which Western countries joined in large numbers.

On the national level, Canada was all the more determined to follow the trend set by other Western countries because of Rwanda. While commanding a UN force there in 1994, General

Roméo Dallaire had been powerless to protect hundreds of thousands of Rwandans from genocide. "Never again," people in Ottawa said. Canada's policy shift on peacekeeping was all the more decisive following the September 11, 2001, terror attacks. Canada joined the United States–led alliance to overturn the Taliban regime in Afghanistan. In 2002, a first battalion of 800 troops was deployed in Kandahar at the same time as special forces and naval and air units took part in anti-terror operations. The tragic attacks of September 11 induced Ottawa to rethink the role of Canada's military in the world. Canadian military wanted to work more closely with their American colleagues. North American defence and the possibility of undertaking joint military operations with the Americans became politically acceptable, relegating peacekeeping operations to the background.

The mission in Afghanistan was the moment many servicemen and women had been waiting for, to show Canadians they could conduct actual combat operations and do something other than just keep the peace.[6] General Rick Hillier, NATO commander in Kabul in 2003–2004, then chief of staff of the Canadian Forces in 2005–2008, symbolized this aspiration. He convinced the Canadian government of the importance of reconfiguring the Canadian Forces to meet new challenges. In this respect, Afghanistan had become a concrete example of conflicts to come: It was a test. As Canada increasingly engaged in this country, it withdrew its troops from other theatres.

The 2005 publication of Canada's International Policy Statement (IPS) reflected the new mandate of the Canadian Forces and Canada's new position in the world. Paul Martin's government didn't renounce its commitment to the UN or peace missions, but emphasized first and foremost its North American relationship, the fight against terrorism, and the military's capability to support expeditionary forces to rebuild fallen states and prevent massacres and genocides.

As soon as the Conservatives took office, they wanted to push things further. They wanted to transform Canada into a warrior nation, and increasingly sought Canadian involvement in multi-lateral missions outside of the UN. This is why they renewed Canada's commitment in Afghanistan in 2008 and got Canada involved in NATO's military operation in Libya in 2011, leading to the overthrow of the government there and the death of Colonel Gaddafi. The Conservative government presented this involvement in a robust military operation as a pivotal moment in Canadian history, and held a big parade in downtown Ottawa saluting the "bravery" of the Canadian Armed Forces.

The militarization of Canadian foreign policy was just one feature of Harper's plan to make Canada a warrior nation. He also wanted to break with the tradition of liberal internationalism, of which peacekeeping operations are a key part. Since Pearson's creation of the Blue Helmets in 1956, Canadians saw themselves as a nation of peacekeepers, of mediators. Some people even believed Canada was a neutral country.

But according to the Conservative prime minister, Canadians only thought like this because previous governments had long concealed Canada's true historical character as a warrior nation. There was something to this. Canada's postwar political and intellectual elites mostly presented Canada as a "good citizen" on the international scene, while minimizing Canada's active involvement in American and Western military strategies. Celebrating the military dimensions of Canadian identity was intended to put things in balance.

But Harper's insistence on Canada being a warrior nation simply got out of hand. By attacking the symbols and achievements of previous governments, the Conservatives were acting like the old Soviet leadership, which had altered photos to remove allies who had suddenly become adversaries. For example, the Conservative government removed the peacekeeping monument from the $10 bill, replacing it with a freight train. The government also refused to mark the 50th anniversary of Pearson's Nobel Peace Prize, and Harper's ministers made a point of never mentioning the former prime minister's name when giving speeches on the highlights of Canadian foreign policy. There was something mean-spirited about this rewriting of history: foreign affairs minister John Baird even removed the name of the "Lester B. Pearson Building" from the ministry address on his business cards.

Some Canadians recognized themselves in the Harper government's warrior nation, but a majority of Canadians were against the intervention in Afghanistan and continued to support peacekeeping. Harper acknowledged public opinion in this respect, and announced the withdrawal of Canadian forces from Afghanistan by 2014. But his government's campaign to discredit peacekeeping turned out to be a complete flop. Canadians, Quebeckers and even proponents of Quebec independence were sharply opposed to the idea of toppling "the Blue Helmet statue."[7]

***

A year before the 2015 elections, members of the International Affairs Council were perfectly aware how deeply embedded the Blue Helmets were in the Canadian public imagination. The Council invited Roland Paris to address the issue, since he had just published a lengthy study analyzing Canadian attitudes to liberal internationalism and Harper's robust foreign policy.[8] Paris pored over a wide range of opinion polls surveying Canadians on their support for the UN and multilateralism, peacekeeping and the more aggressive role Harper wanted for the Canadian Armed Forces.

The Conservative campaign against the UN and the Blue Helmets was having some impact: The data overall showed a decline in Canadians' support for these institutions. But a strong majority of Canadians still had high regard for the UN, and for peacekeeping in particular. The results showed that Canadians accepted a more aggressive role for their Armed Forces, without necessarily being in favour of militarism. Paris noted in conclusion that "after eight years of Conservative government, Canadians continue to express an overwhelming preference for the liberal internationalist role over Prime Minister Harper's alternative."[9]

According to Paris, Canadians wanted their country to return to peacekeeping operations, even if they knew this would involve the loss of Canadian lives. In this sense, Canadians had a realistic view of peacekeeping missions that were now deployed in conflict zones where peace was fragile or nonexistent. Since the UN couldn't bring military force to bear on such situations, other international organizations had to fill the breach: NATO in Kosovo and in Afghanistan; the African Union in Somalia; the European Union in Chad.

Based on Paris's study and the new realities of peacekeeping, the International Affairs Council presented Trudeau with a series of proposals to re-engage Canada in peace operations. The Council suggested offering the UN special means for supporting its missions, as well as mediation specialists. Along with several other Council members, I proposed reflecting on what would be needed to develop a rapid reaction force able to intervene in the initial stage of a deployment, and to set up a training structure for military, police and civilians taking part in peacekeeping operations. I also drew my colleagues' attention to the patterns of conflict in French-speaking Africa, where only eleven of twenty-five francophone countries enjoyed stability. As a member of La Francophonie, Canada had a responsibility to address this problem, since it had the human and material resources to help the countries concerned. These suggestions all found their way into the Liberal Party program, and they were all incorporated in the new peacekeeping policy unveiled in summer 2016.

***

Minister Stéphane Dion was particularly interested in peacekeeping. This was the main reason he appointed me as his political adviser. From day one, he asked me to work on this file and to draft several speeches on peacekeeping. Several ministries were involved in developing Canada's new strategy of re-engagement in peacekeeping operations, notably Foreign Affairs, National Defence and Public Safety, as well as the Prime Minister's Office. In Minister Dion's office, I worked on the strategy along with the policy director, Christopher Berzins. We brought a political perspective and new ideas to the work of the public servants at Foreign Affairs.

In May and in June 2016, teams of public servants at Foreign Affairs and National Defence worked on two complementary projects: the re-engagement strategy and the creation of a program to fund Canadian and foreign projects related to peacekeeping operations. Creating this latter program was no problem, since it would be funded by Foreign Affairs. But the re-engagement strategy led to conflicts between the minister's office and civil servants at Foreign Affairs, and also between Foreign Affairs and National Defence. The Prime Minister's Office stood on the sidelines during this stage of the strategy's development.

During a meeting with public servants at Foreign Affairs, I recommended they keep features of Trudeau's election program in mind. They didn't warm to this kind of suggestion, but the fact was the government had been elected to implement a program. They discussed my recommendation with their colleagues at National Defence. The first draft of the re-engagement strategy incorporated some features of the election platform: providing the UN with military and police contingents, specialized personnel and equipment; launching an initiative for the training of civilian and military personnel; supporting mediation, conflict prevention and reconstruction efforts. The public servants added other proposals, such as developing measures to protect civilians; promoting the role of women and girls in peace processes; and supporting strategies to strengthen fragile States.

I liked this first draft, but Berzins felt something was missing. He proposed an early warning system that would detect conflicts before they blew up, opening the way to preventive interventions. The public servants balked at this proposal, which they rightfully deemed unrealistic.

It was hard to set up an early warning system, and in any case this included interfering in another country's internal affairs. Recognizing conflicts early on meant setting up some elements of the early warning system on the ground in the country concerned. The local government was likely to reject any foreign intrusion. The international system is based on respect for national sovereignty, so any foreign intrusion would be construed as a violation of sovereignty. But Berzins defended the idea, saying the time had come for concrete action to prevent conflicts. The civil servants gave in.

In this first draft, Berzins and I noticed National Defence had not scoped out its contributions of personnel or equipment. Things were left vague. We met with Minister Dion to discuss the first draft of the strategy. Dion asked why Defence was not putting a dollar amount on its contributions. I suggested the military were not particularly enthusiastic about peace operations, and preferred taking part in NATO missions or joining multinational coalitions along with the United States. As a matter of fact, just as we were defining Canada's re-engagement with the UN, National Defence was discussing the deployment of Canadian military in Latvia with the Prime Minister's Office, in line with NATO's 2014 decision to counter the Russian threat in the Baltic region.

I pointed out to the minister that National Defence had calculated the cost of sending military personnel to Latvia down to the last dollar. In my opinion, they were waiting for approval of the deployment in Latvia before committing to peacekeeping operations.

Finally, in July 2016, the Latvia deployment got the green light. This broke the deadlock in our discussions on peacekeeping operations, and National Defence could now calculate its contribution of personnel and equipment. Things were all set to announce the policy of re-engagement in peacekeeping.

On August 26, 2016, the government rolled out the red carpet. Four ministers attended the press conference: Foreign Affairs, National Defence, International Development and Public Safety. The policy had three components: a document called "Canada's Reengagement in UN Peacekeeping," which laid out peacekeeping policy over the next few years; a five-year renewal of the International Police Peacekeeping Program, providing for Canada's deployment of up to 150 police officers in military theatres; and finally, creation of the Peace and Stabilization Operations Program, with $150 million in annual funding for each of the next three years: This program was tasked with supporting conflict prevention, mediation, dialogue and reconciliation initiatives, improving the effectiveness of peacekeeping operations, supporting fragile states and responding rapidly to crises.

National Defence took advantage of the press conference to confirm it was ready to deploy up to 600 members of the Canadian Armed Forces in UN peace operations. Everything was ready, except for one thing: Where exactly did the government want to send Canada's military and police contribution? This was the point at which everything came to a standstill.

***

The commitment to re-engage in UN peacekeeping operations was an important part of the Liberal Party of Canada's program.[10] This commitment also featured during the 2015 election campaign. Since the end of the Second World War, peacekeeping had served as the most eloquent illustration of liberal internationalism — the principle Canada's political establishment liked using to highlight Canada's unique role on the international scene. In many respects, the Blue Helmet had become a Canadian symbol just as much as the beaver or maple leaf. But during their decade in office, the Conservatives had abandoned this symbol. They wanted Canada to join multinational coalitions with the United States instead, and to wage war. This, of course, was not to the liking of Trudeau and the Liberals.

Members of the International Affairs Council were unanimously in favour of Canada's re-engaging with peacekeeping operations. During the session on May 2, 2014, we met with the Liberal leader to discuss the crisis in the Central African Republic, where the UN warned genocide was about to happen. I reminded my colleagues that Canada knew the situation on the ground well, since it had already taken part in a UN mission there in 1998. We Council members agreed that Canada should take part in a mission there if the Liberal Party formed the next government.

The policy of re-engagement announced in August 2016 resulted directly from discussions of the Council. The announcement that 600 military personnel and 150 police officers would be provided indicated Canada was planning a significant commitment to peacekeeping operations. This was, moreover, the direction that preparatory work on deployment options in Africa was taking through fall 2016 — work involving civil servants at National Defence, Foreign Affairs and Public Safety as well as advisers in the respective ministers' offices. Six major UN peacekeeping operations were then deployed in Africa: in Ivory Coast, Darfur, Mali, the Central African Republic, South Sudan and the Democratic Republic of the Congo. We quickly chose to set aside the first two missions on the list, concentrating instead on the four others, because these were difficult missions where the UN needed solid material and political support from member states, especially industrial countries with the heavy equipment and specialized contingents needed to carry out particular tasks.

In-depth analyses were undertaken on these four peacekeeping operations. Defence minister Harjit Sajjan and international development minister Marie-Claude Bibeau went to a few of these places to see first-hand how the operations were going. Civil servants and military personnel spent several weeks in Africa doing technical evaluations of each of the peacekeeping operations and holding political discussions with the different actors in the countries concerned: governments, representatives of civil society, commanding officers of peacekeeping forces and diplomats from Western countries.

The Canadian civil servants brought all of this evidence together to develop an accurate, in-depth assessment of each of the four peacekeeping operations to determine whether Canada should get involved in each one. This assessment was based on seven criteria: whether Canada could have a real impact on the situation and strengthen the capabilities of the UN; whether it would promote Canada's interests (commercial or geopolitical); whether it would limit the security risks for Canadian Blue Helmets; whether deployment would provide good diplomatic visibility; whether peacekeeping training would include knowledge transfer; whether Canada would focus on areas where it had comparative advantages; and finally, whether Canada would influence peace processes.

The civil servants then worked out four deployment scenarios, each of which included small-scale, mid-sized and large-scale commitments. The large-scale deployment proposed for Mali was everyone's favourite: It incorporated a military and police presence there, as well as development, diplomatic and reconstruction features, and finally the protection of women and girls in that country. Berzins and I familiarized ourselves with these scenarios and then held discussions with our counterparts at National Defence before approving them. Minister Dion and the defence minister got a complete briefing before a meeting on December 1, 2016, with fellow ministers on the Cabinet Committee on International Affairs. The night before, at midnight, I prepared Dion's notes for his colleagues. Dion outlined the different scenarios and the committee gave its approval. The time had now come to inform the prime minister. Meanwhile, at the UN, the Secretary General's Office was planning to name a francophone Canadian general to head the Mission in Mali (MINUSMA).

Everything was ready for the meeting to get Trudeau's approval.

Suddenly, the prime minister's inner circle panicked. Things were going too fast, people in his office said. Some advisers wanted to make sure they understood the various scenarios. They preferred delaying any announcement of Canada's peacekeeping deployment until January 2017. Then on Thursday, December 15, after days of discussions between the ministers' offices and the Prime Minister's Office, Trudeau met with the chief of staff of the Armed Forces, General Jonathan Vance, for a two-hour briefing on the different scenarios and the proposed deployment in Mali. The prime minister expressed his satisfaction. He planned to discuss the matter at a Cabinet meeting at the end of January, after the holidays. The UN was ready to delay naming a Canadian general to command MINUSMA. But then on January 6, 2017, came a dramatic development: Trudeau fired Dion.

***

On February 10, 2017, I left the office of the new minister, Chrystia Freeland. Her chief of staff informed me that the files I had been working on — multilateralism, peacekeeping and Africa — would not be priorities for the minister. She would be devoting all her energies to relations with the United States and renegotiating the North American Free Trade Agreement.

In other words, re-engaging with peace operations had been put on the back burner. In fact, up to the Vancouver announcement in November 2017, the Prime Minister's Office had played ping-pong with Foreign Affairs and National Defence on this file. Clearly, Trudeau's advisers had convinced him to reject the proposed scenarios, and they were now asking for something new and less ambitious. The reason for this turn of events involved political, financial and security considerations. The prime minister and his advisers now lacked the political will to commit Canada to conflict resolution. And the UN was entangled in conflicts that were both violent and complicated.

In this respect, the case of Mali was instructive. The country was facing terrorist attacks and a difficult process of national reconciliation. France was charged with the security of the country and the regime, but was variously liked and detested by the Malian people and part of the country's elites. This was therefore a complex situation, and the prime minister and his advisers saw no way out of the crisis.

Moreover, the proposed deployment in Mali would be expensive. The different options varied by several hundred million dollars. Just when the government was planning to increase the deficit, a new commitment to this deployment would put it in an uncomfortable position. Finally, the mission would pose considerable risks for Canadian Blue Helmets deployed there. Afghanistan continued to haunt the government and many Canadians. Over a decade, Canada had lost about 160 Armed Forces members in Afghanistan. The UN mission in Mali couldn't be compared to the NATO mission in Afghanistan, but more than a hundred Blue Helmets had died in Mali since 2014. Trudeau retreated on the issue. He was afraid of the risks. In his mind, there could be no question of deploying a contingent of Canadians there. This message was forwarded to the UN and on March 2 a Belgian general was appointed commander of MINUSMA.

Now that the large-scale scenarios had been rejected, the prime minister sought a way to save face. The Vancouver ministerial conference was around the corner, and Canada still had nothing to offer. Trudeau's advisers asked the civil servants to develop cheaper and less risky scenarios. Over the next few months, the civil servants came back with half a dozen options, all of which proved unacceptable to the Prime Minister's Office.

By the end of the summer of 2017, in the final weeks leading up to the ministerial conference in Vancouver, civil servants at Foreign Affairs and National Defence were increasingly nervous. They contacted the Prime Minister's Office again; it came back with a highly unusual request. The PMO asked the civil servants not to focus on any specific deployment, but to map out a generic involvement in UN peace operations instead, by providing a transport plane or a few helicopters or a training program.

The civil servants were astonished by this request. For a year now, they had been discussing with their counterparts in the United States, Europe, Africa and at the UN the ambitious prospect of Canada's military and police deployment in one or two peace operations. These other parties all expected the deployment to take place. But then the prime minister changed his mind, backing away from the risks and abandoning Canada's allies.

At the Vancouver conference, the prime minister presented Canada's contribution in re-engaging with peace operations. This contribution was the result of urgent, last-minute consultations held just as the conference got under way. The contribution would be modest and have two features. One was funding of specific programs likely to be implemented in Canada or abroad: $24 million to modernize peace operations and increase the number of women deployed in missions; an unspecified sum for a program to prevent the recruitment and use of child soldiers; and finally, a training program to improve a partner country's contribution.

The second feature of the contribution involved the supply of equipment and the deployment of personnel. Canada was ready to respond to UN requests. It was offering the UN a transport plane, a few helicopters and a rapid intervention force. But this second contribution wasn't actually a firm commitment. Every commitment had to be negotiated separately, and the Canadian government reserved the right to go back on its word whenever it wanted.

The prime minister introduced this contribution as an innovative and modern approach intended to improve peace operations.[11] It was nothing of the kind. Canada had not taken part in any UN peace operations since the mission to Ethiopia and Eritrea in 2000. Needless to say, the 124 other countries that had contributed to the Blue Helmets since 2000 hadn't waited around for Canada to come up with innovations or proposals to update peace operations. Over the last decade and a half, the UN had undertaken several reforms of its peace operations with a view to improving their management, deployment and effectiveness. Canadian proposals aimed at preventing recruitment of child soldiers, deploying more women on missions and forming contingents of participating countries were useful, but hardly ground-breaking.

Nobody was impressed by the announcement in Vancouver of Canada's new commitment to peace operations. At the UN, the Secretary General and the representatives of UN peace operations were disappointed.

But that wasn't the end of the story. In a surprise move on March 19, 2018, the government announced deployment within the UN mission in Mali (MINUSMA) of a contingent of Blue Helmets comprising a unit of six helicopters and a logistical support group.

Clearly, the prime minister had given in to pressure from abroad and from within Cabinet. Justin Trudeau could be bold in taking foreign policy decisions, but usually he was reactive rather than proactive. He hesitated; he dithered; he was inclined to change course. In the case of the Mali mission, quickly developing events in March forced him to act. Several allied countries with troops in Mali, among them Germany, France and the Netherlands, exerted strong pressure on Canada to get it to join the peacekeeping effort there. Germany in particular needed another country to step in and replace its own helicopters on the ground there.

There was increasing discontent within the government. Several people at Foreign Affairs pointed out that Canada was absent from the international scene just when it was in the final stages of preparing the G7 summit in Charlevoix, slated for June 2018. Some of the G7 countries had contingents of Blue Helmets overseas. As usual, the prime minister waffled. His close advisers were split on the issue, with some favouring Canadian deployment in UN peace operations and others opposing it. Finally, everything played out during the week of March 12. After several telephone conversations between the heads of the Canadian, German and Dutch governments, Canada finally agreed to provide the UN with equipment and personnel for the mission in Mali, but for one year only. The whole contingent would be withdrawn by the summer of 2019.

This planned contribution would be limited. Canada would play no role in the Malian peace process itself. And in so doing, Canada relinquished one of its traditional roles — involvement in conflict resolution.

PART 3
CANADA AND THE WORLD'S MAJOR PLAYERS

CHAPTER NINE

UKRAINE'S INFLUENCE ON CANADA'S RUSSIA POLICY

Ukraine occupied a disproportionate place in Canadian foreign policy for a dozen years, to the point that it prevented Canada from articulating and implementing a Russia policy based on geopolitics and the defence of its own national interests.

Wedged between Russia and Europe, Ukraine gained independence in 1991 with the collapse of the Soviet Union. Canada was one of the first countries to recognize Ukraine. The two nations quickly developed close relations, particularly under the influence of 1.3 million Canadians of Ukrainian origin, most of whom live in the Western provinces. Ukrainians had deep roots in Canada going back to the end of the nineteenth century and are well integrated into Canadian society. Several federal MPs and members of provincial legislatures are of Ukrainian origin.

In 2004, the Ukrainian question featured prominently in the Canadian media and political landscape during a controversial election campaign in Ukraine pitting a pro-Russian party against a group of pro-Western parties. Canada sent a large delegation of election monitors led by former Prime Minister John Turner. The pro-Western parties managed to win the election, but political tensions persisted in Ukraine. Several years later, the pro-Russian party regained power.

With each election, Canada interfered increasingly in the internal affairs of the country, citing its need to "monitor elections" there. During the presidential elections of 2010 and the general elections of 2012, large contingents of Canadian monitors turned up in Ukraine. The Canadian International Development Agency (CIDA) funded these delegations, noting that they increasingly comprised Canadians of Ukrainian origin.[1] Many of these delegates had no prior experience of election monitoring and were perceived as favouring pro-Western parties in Ukraine.

CIDA recommended that the Canadian government do election monitoring along with the Organization for Security and Co-operation in Europe, a respected institution with an impressive track record in this area. At the time, Stephen Harper flatly rejected CIDA's recommendations.

Harper's position on the Ukrainian question was rooted in values, geopolitics and domestic political calculations. The former prime minister remembered Ukraine's suffering under communism and particularly during Stalin's rule, when millions of Ukrainians died during the Soviet-made famine of the 1930s and thousands of political prisoners were executed.

The former prime minister truly disliked the Soviet Union. He didn't think much more of the New Russia, especially now that Vladimir Putin was in power. The Kremlin's increasingly brutal reign under Putin followed a chaotic period under Boris Yeltsin. For Harper, Putin's methods at the Kremlin were incompatible with Western values. Moreover, Harper recognized the threat Russia posed for Europe: He was disturbed by Russia's vengeful and aggressive position in its war with Georgia in 2008, and Moscow's attempts to influence political life in several former Soviet republics such as Moldova, Uzbekistan and Estonia.

Finally, and no doubt most importantly, Harper supported Ukraine as a way of shoring up votes in the all-important Ukrainian community in Canada.

During the Russia-Ukraine crisis of 2014, this electoral bias came to the fore. In December 2013, the pro-Russian government in Ukraine rejected association with the European Union and moved closer to Moscow instead, leading to a storm of protest from pro-Western parties and movements. Thousands of protesters stormed the centre of the capital, Kiev, paralyzing the economic and political life of the country. Canadian foreign affairs minister John Baird went to Kiev and interfered directly in the internal affairs of the country by openly supporting the protesters. In February, many people were killed during anti-government demonstrations, and the president ended up fleeing the country. A pro-Western government was established. Moscow denounced this reversal as a coup d'état, holding Washington and Europe responsible. Western countries saw it as a revolution instead.

Putin had feared this moment for a long time. He moved quickly, seizing and annexing Crimea, a predominantly Russian region handed to Ukraine by Nikita Khrushchev in 1954. At the same time, he used pro-Russian rebellions in Eastern Ukraine against the new government to add fuel to the fire. These events confirmed Harper's worst suspicions about Russia and led to a freeze in relations with Putin's regime, along with the adoption of economic sanctions against Russia.

The Ukrainian crisis is still having a negative impact on relations between Russia and the West. While the media continue covering each episode of the conflict, the root of the crisis lies in Russia's geopolitical struggle with NATO countries for control of the former Soviet bloc.

***

Canada's membership in NATO is one of the pillars of this country's foreign and defence policy. The Atlantic Alliance was founded in 1949 to counter the Soviet Union's aggressive moves in postwar Europe. Canada was a founding member. Lester B. Pearson and other leading Canadian diplomats helped draft the NATO Charter, which provides for the collective defence of European and North American members.

"The enemy was in the East," but NATO's political and military role went beyond mere opposition to the Soviet Union. According to the rather cynical formulation of Lord Ismay, first secretary general of the organization, NATO's essential role was "to keep the Soviet Union out, the Americans in, and the Germans down."[2] This is as true today as it was in 1949.

NATO has evolved over time, undertaking combat missions (Afghanistan) and peacekeeping missions (Bosnia, Kosovo) under a UN mandate. After the fall of communism, NATO membership has expanded into Eastern Europe and now reaches right up to the Russian border, removing the buffer zone between East and West. This proximity has soured relations between Moscow and the West for about twenty years. According to Moscow, the West has simply reneged on a commitment made to Gorbachev during negotiations on German reunification in 1989–1990, a commitment not to expand NATO up to the Russian border.

According to Washington, no such undertaking was ever made to Moscow. Who is right? It is hard to say, although historical research tends to side with Gorbachev. Negotiations at the time involved the American, European and Soviet leadership. Everything indicates the Russians grudgingly accepted that NATO expand into Poland, Hungary and the Czech Republic. But they did not want NATO expanding right up to the Russian border, whether in the Baltic states or eventually Ukraine. Any such move would be a red line for Moscow.

Canada was not involved in these negotiations. Former Prime Minister Mulroney didn't mention the issue in his memoirs. At best he gave a speech at Stanford University in 1991, stating that Eastern European countries should become part of NATO "if they adopted democratic governance and values."[3] Initially, his proposal shocked the British. Why? He didn't say more. But it was too early to talk about expanding NATO membership, and Mulroney left power two years later.

On taking office in 1993, Chrétien inherited this extremely delicate file. He was well aware of Russian opposition to expanded NATO membership, but the following year in Brussels he proposed welcoming three new Eastern European democracies into the Alliance. The reasons Chrétien invoked were eclectic, if not completely frivolous: Romania "because of its purchase of our CANDU nuclear reactors . . . ; Ukraine, because of the one million Canadians of Ukrainian origin; and Slovenia" at the urging of its prime minister.[4] When NATO admitted a first group of new members in 1999, it completely ignored Chrétien's proposal: None of these three countries acceded to the Alliance. During subsequent debates with NATO allies, Chrétien invoked moral reasons, citing the three countries' adoption of democracy and market economies.

The most surprising thing in Mulroney's and Chrétien's memoirs is their complete lack of reflection on the consequences of NATO's expansion to the East. The two former prime ministers didn't consider strategic issues or Russia's interests with respect to NATO enlargement. They didn't foresee any future consequences of NATO's move. Chrétien dismissed the matter as little more than a petty quarrel: "There will never come a day when the Russians are happy about the expansion of NATO," he writes. "They will be as angry in ten years as now, so we might as well do what will have to be done some day."

And yet, in the years ahead, NATO's expansion widened the breach between NATO and Moscow. In 2007, Putin gave a speech at a conference in Munich on international security, slamming American hegemony and NATO expansion, which he saw as going against Russian interests:

> *"I think it is obvious that NATO expansion does
> not have any relation with the modernization of
> the Alliance itself or with ensuring security in
> Europe. On the contrary, it represents a serious
> provocation that reduces the level of mutual trust.
> And we have the right to ask: against whom is
> this expansion intended? And what happened to
> the assurances our Western partners made after
> the dissolution of the Warsaw Pact? Where are
> those declarations today? No one even remembers
> them."*[5]

But in 2008, NATO ignored Russia again, opening the door to eventually admitting Georgia and Ukraine to the Alliance. This time, Putin denounced the move as a direct threat to Russia.

***

The Liberals faced this delicate geopolitical situation upon gaining power in 2015. Dion was somewhat ambivalent about NATO. He acknowledged the Alliance was a pillar of the security architecture of both Canada and Western countries. But he saw NATO expansion towards the East as an error, beyond Poland, Hungary and the Czech Republic acceding to the Alliance. He also thought NATO took an extremely aggressive attitude towards Russia. I completely shared his point of view. We didn't see eye to eye on this issue with civil servants at Foreign Affairs, who all blindly accepted that NATO was intrinsically a force for good. In April 2016, Dion and I met the civil servants responsible for the Alliance in the lead-up to the next NATO summit in Brussels, which would be held a few weeks later. Several countries, including Canada, were planning to announce they were strengthening

NATO's presence in the Baltic countries to help them stand up to Russia.

The civil servants presented the minister with a document about the main issues of the summit and an assessment of the Russian "threat." They also presented details of a NATO proposal that Canada lead a multinational contingent in Latvia. The document was couched in the warlike language the Pentagon and NATO typically used towards Russia.

I asked the civil servants what they thought of this document and the assessment of the "threat." They answered that they trusted their sources. I wasn't surprised by this response. What else could they say? The Americans and British assessed the Russian "threat," and Canada had no way of validating the assessment independently. Besides, had the Canadian civil servants really tried to verify this information? For more than sixty-five years, the English-speaking members of NATO (the United States, the United Kingdom and sometimes Canada) had imposed their reading of the international situation on all the other members. This was obvious to any well-informed observer of international relations. "You have to see a NATO summit for yourself to realize the stranglehold the American military have on the organization," writes Dominique de Villepin, former French minister of foreign affairs.[6]

A few minutes before meeting with the civil servants, I went to let Dion know I disagreed with this assessment of the Russian "threat" and the proposal that Canada lead a multinational contingent. I thought there was no military justification for this deployment and it would only add fuel to the fire. Putin could create trouble in Georgia and Ukraine, two countries outside of NATO, I told the minister, but he understood that any intervention in a NATO country could spark a crisis or even a war. I suggested our contribution be symbolic instead. Our military would prove more useful on a peacekeeping mission in Africa than in a Baltic country.

The minister disagreed with my view of the deployment in Latvia, but he still didn't like the document, especially since it had little to say about NATO's political and diplomatic relations with Russia. He got angry, asking the civil servants why the document had a lot to say about military measures but nothing about diplomacy, which Canada and many other countries had specifically asked for. "I am reminding you this is a new government, and we want to change the tone and political character of our relations with Russia," he told them. He asked them to redraft the entire document and drop any martial language.

A few days later, we received a new version of the document. The warlike rhetoric had been removed and the document now highlighted diplomatic aspects of Canada's relations with Russia. The tone was more diplomatic, but the substance was the same as before: Canada agreed to lead a multinational contingent in Latvia, providing 450 Canadian members of the Armed Forces. I had lost this battle, said Christopher Berzins, Dion's policy director.

NATO came back to haunt us at the beginning of October 2016. The Atlantic Treaty Association had invited Minister Dion to address its annual meeting in Toronto. At Foreign Affairs, the minister, the civil servants and I had vigorous debates about what the speech should say. Dion asked me to write a first draft. I quickly submitted a draft containing all the elements of classical NATO rhetoric. However, after a few paragraphs, I moved the speech in another direction, highlighting our commitment to conflict resolution by means of multilateralism and peace operations. I stressed that NATO was not the only organization Canada depended on to ensure world peace. We also counted on the United Nations, which explained why Trudeau was committing to re-engage Canada in peace operations. Dion was happy with the speech, but he had a problem with the phrase "NATO, a factor for peace." He asked me to change this to "NATO, a catalyst for peace." This of course didn't amount to the same thing, and the minister wanted to make sure people knew about it.

The speech was ready; the minister flew to Toronto. But things took a sudden turn. The assistant deputy minister responsible for international security got hold of the speech and objected to its overall thrust as well as to the reference to peace operations. And since he was attending the same conference and staying at the same hotel, he intercepted the minister to push for major changes.

The new version placed NATO front and centre and celebrated its virtues, although the assistant deputy minister kept a few paragraphs on multilateralism and Canada's return to peace operations. He reminded the minister that the audience expected Canada to make a strong statement on NATO. Dion would not be swayed and rejected the new version. He said Canada's commitment to NATO was a matter of public knowledge and there was no need to repeat it endlessly. He came back to the first draft of the speech with a few minor changes.[7]

***

Putin's Russia is anything but a Western-style democracy. Opposition parties are weak. Freedom of expression is severely restricted. Most media serve the government. The regime controls the levers of executive, legislative and judicial power. Opponents are assassinated under murky circumstances. While it is true the Russian economy is no bigger than Australia's, Russia counts on the international scene. It has an impressive nuclear arsenal rivalling that of the United States, and its conventional military capabilities are formidable.

Russia has few military bases abroad, unlike the United States and France, which are present around the world. But Russia is able to exert direct influence in conflict situations, as shown by its intervention in Syria since 2015. Finally, on the diplomatic level, Russia exerts considerable influence as a permanent member of the UN Security Council and through its presence in all international organizations and forums.

Canada cannot ignore Russia. With the United States to the south, Russia to the north is Canada's only other big neighbour. Relations between Canada and Russia were established in 1941. Since that time, they have gone through two distinct periods. The first, lasting up to the 1991 breakup of the Soviet Union into fifteen independent republics, was marked by more episodic than continuous relations, and was impacted by the Cold War and détente. Relations were based on geopolitics more than economic interests or shared values. In 1955, Pearson was the first among ministers of foreign affairs of a NATO member to go to the Soviet Union and confer with the new leadership replacing Stalin. He tried establishing dialogue and reducing East–West tensions. Relations between the two countries reached a low point during the worst crises of the Cold War — the Soviet invasion of Hungary in 1956 and the Cuban missile crisis in 1962. Things only began to change once Pierre Trudeau took office.

Trudeau was more open to improving relations with the USSR than his predecessors had been. He was less rigid ideologically, and he could take advantage of a unique international dynamic. East–West relations were thawing thanks to the policy of détente promoted by American president Richard Nixon and German chancellor Willy Brandt. Contacts between Canadian and Soviet leaders increased. Economic exchanges increased, and soon Soviet-built Ladas could be seen on the streets of Montreal.

Hockey became a vital part of relations between the two countries, with the Canada–Soviet Summit Series in 1972, played in four Canadian cities and one Soviet city. In 1983, Mikhail Gorbachev, then the little-known Soviet minister of agriculture, visited Canada for three weeks. He discovered the strong industrial and economic performance of Canada's agricultural sector, a part of whose production was then exported to his own country. Gorbachev is said to have been convinced during this official visit to push for the economic liberalization and democratization of the Soviet Union, which he did on becoming the new leader of that country two years later.

Brian Mulroney and Jean Chrétien improved relations with Moscow, especially in economic terms. During their time as prime minister, both led large groups of business people on important trade missions there. At the same time, they did everything they could to welcome Russia into the community of nations after the collapse of the Soviet Union. This marks the second period in relations between Canada and Russia. Chrétien in particular worked tirelessly to include Russia in Western forums. At the G7 summit in Halifax in 1995, Chrétien invited Boris Yeltsin to sit at the table, and nobody objected.[8] It was only in 1998 that Russia officially joined the group of industrialized nations, which then became known as the G8. But after Russia's intervention in Ukraine in 2014, it was no longer to be invited to G8 summits.[9]

Relations between Russia and Canada certainly had their ups and downs over a twenty-year period, but in one area, these relations were unavoidable: the Arctic. In his day, Pierre Trudeau highlighted the importance of the Arctic in Foreign Policy for Canadians, a 1970 government document defining new priorities for Canadian diplomacy. In justifying improved relations with Moscow, Trudeau cited the fact that "Canada shares the experience of being an Arctic country" with the Soviet Union.[10] The Arctic was still front and centre in Canadian political discourse seventeen years later, but for quite another reason: the new Soviet threat.

In 1987, the Conservative government tabled a far more alarmist white paper on defence. According to the document,

Canada now faced a new threat from Moscow, especially since "Canadian Arctic waters could well provide an alternate route for Soviet submarines to move from the Arctic Ocean to reach" the American northeast coast and "attack vital Allied shipping."[11]

Apart from the Soviet threat, Canada also had to take care of defending its sovereignty. And in the Arctic, this sovereignty was threatened most of all by . . . the United States. The two countries disputed the status of the Northwest Passage. For Ottawa, this passage was part of Canada's territorial waters, meaning any ship needed to seek authorization before traversing the passage. Washington considered it to be an international strait and therefore no Canadian authorization was needed.

In view of this dual threat — both Soviet and American — and Canada's international responsibilities, the document continued, the government was planning to acquire nuclear-powered submarines.[12] The idea seemed bold, but it failed to materialize. Two years later, in April 1989, the Conservative government cancelled the submarine acquisition program, because Canada was now facing an economic downturn. The decision was taken even before the fall of the Berlin Wall in November of that year and the disappearance of the Soviet threat.

***

Nowadays, under Justin Trudeau, the Arctic is making the news once again. The region is becoming more central to international relations, stirring competition between Nordic countries such as Russia and Canada for several distinct reasons: the rapid melting of sea ice, the Northwest Passage, natural resources, security, the environment and Indigenous rights. Indeed, the Arctic is not just made up of islands and lands: It is also a sea on the point of becoming a route for maritime traffic, presenting potential consequences for the environment, legal challenges and the prospect of geopolitical tensions. China, a new superpower, entered the fray in September 2017, requesting Ottawa's authorization for the sole Chinese icebreaker to traverse the Northwest Passage.

Unlike Antarctica, the Arctic falls outside of all international legal regimes.[13] Eight countries consider themselves Arctic nations and exercise their sovereignty over the waters and icepack of this region. For this reason, these Arctic nations created a high-level intergovernmental forum in 1991, the Arctic Council, to address issues relating to the environment, the rights of Indigenous peoples and sustainable development. The Council does not address military issues. Six Indigenous associations sit on the Council as permanent members, and a dozen other countries attend meetings as observer states.

Russia's immense polar territory guarantees it a central place in the Arctic. In fact, Russia dominates this region of the world, whereas the United States is relegated to a secondary role.[14] Russia maintains a constellation of land and naval bases in this geographical space, as well as much of its fleet of nuclear submarines. Russia projects heavy military power in the Arctic.[15] It has rich reserves of oil, gas and mineral ores in the region, although harsh conditions make extraction difficult and pose potential hazards for the environment. Human activity here seems to be advancing as the ice gradually retreats. This acceleration of activity preoccupies all Nordic nations — above all, Canada.

By the time the Liberals came to power in 2015, relations between Canada and Russia were very poor. They had suffered as a result of the Russian military intervention in Ukraine a year earlier and Western retaliatory sanctions slapped on Russia. The two countries limited their interactions considerably, even restricting visits by civil servants. Dion was deeply troubled by the situation and wondered how to change things.

Dion was a university professor at heart — a born teacher. He was convinced that reason, not passion, should dictate the course of relations with Russia. He therefore sought new dialogue with Moscow based on a policy of openness and a realistic appraisal of the interests of the two countries. Three months after being named minister, Dion defined the line for the Trudeau government to follow towards difficult regimes: "Speaking to regimes we disagree with is necessary if we want to make progress. To dislike a regime is one thing. To refuse to speak with it and still think progress is possible is a mistake."[16] Dion was clearly referring to Russia as well as Iran and North Korea.

In another speech two months later, Dion articulated the guiding principles of Canadian foreign policy. He and I worked together on the speech, to be given at the University of Ottawa, defining the philosophical underpinnings of the Trudeau government's foreign policy and its application in specific cases such as Russia. On this occasion, Dion laid out his principle of "responsible conviction," as noted above in chapter four. Canada defended its commitment to freedom, democracy, human rights, and equality between men and women, while taking into account the consequences of Canadian actions in a highly imperfect world. Canada must be responsible. As Canada faced the world, it must engage with the world with its eyes open, not withdraw from it.

Russia was a case where responsible conviction should be applied. Dion conceded that current relations with Russia were poor, but they had also been poor during the Cold War. Dion drew a parallel between the two eras, reminding his listeners that even during the Cold War, Canada continued speaking to the Soviet Union, a country with an authoritarian regime. And this dialogue turned out to be beneficial.

"Under the 'disengagement' policy of the Harper government, it would have been impossible to organize the 1972 Summit Series between Canada and the USSR . . . which helped build cultural and people-to-people ties during a time of great tension."[17] Moreover, "it would have been impossible to invite a young

Mikhail Gorbachev to Canada in 1983 . . . It was in Ontario and Alberta that Gorbachev first came to see the great inefficiencies of the Soviet agricultural system compared to ours," Dion said.

Dialogue opens up new windows of opportunity. In the case of Gorbachev's visit, it planted the seeds for a true democratic revolution in Russia. It also kept channels of communication open, benefiting all parties, particularly Ukraine. "Canada's severing of ties with Russia had no positive consequences for anyone: not for Canadians, not for the Russian people, not for Ukraine, and not for global security," Dion reminded his audience whenever he could.[18]

But there was more. Dialogue with Russia was necessary and unavoidable because a country like Canada needed to defend its own vital interests. The Arctic provided a good example of this fact, and Dion frequently returned to the theme to drive home his point about openness. Many experts noted that Canada and Russia had mutual interests to protect in the Arctic region.

Before the Ukrainian crisis, Michael Byers of the University of British Columbia, one of the country's top Arctic specialists, spoke of a "Canada–Russia Axis" in the region. The two countries took similar views on the sovereignty of the Northwest Passage north of Canada and the Northeast Passage north of Russia. "Canada considers the Northwest Passage to be internal waters. Russia takes the same view of the Northern Sea Route." Besides, in 1982, the two countries worked together on drafting the United Nations Convention on the Law of the Sea, codifying the right of coastal states to exercise regulatory power over shipping traffic in ice-covered zones.[19]

On September 29, 2016, in marking the 20th anniversary of the Arctic Council's creation, Dion pursued the same theme of improving Canada's relations with Russia. After reviewing the challenges all eight Council members faced, the minister singled out Russia, and for good reason. "Let's insist on the crucial relationship that must exist between Canada and Russia. Almost 50 percent of the North is Russian, and some 25 percent is Canadian. Between us we control 75 percent of the North."[20]

Dion then invoked his guiding principle of "responsible conviction" to promote Canada's engagement with the Russians. "Cooperation with Russia on the full range of Arctic issues is simply in our best interests," he said. "When I met with Minister Lavrov in July, we made Arctic cooperation a priority. It can be no other way." And the Arctic Council is a forum for consensus. No consensus is possible without Canada and Russia working together, as difficult as that may be at times.

***

Dion's determination to restore relations with Russia quickly came up against pro-Ukrainian pressure groups. These groups were organized around the Ukrainian Canadian Congress founded in 1940, MPs and senators of all parties represented in Parliament, as well as several small organizations, some of them set up following Ukraine's independence in 1991 or in the aftermath of the Russian attack on Ukraine in 2014. They also received the support of about 1.3 million Canadians of Ukrainian origin living mainly in the Western provinces.

Among the parliamentarians, Foreign Affairs minister Chrystia Freeland stood out as a pro-Ukrainian activist. In July 2014, a few months after being elected MP, she cited her own Ukrainian origins as a reason the Liberal Party should take a strong stand in favour of Ukraine and against Russia. As a member of Trudeau's International Affairs Council, I immediately wrote to the Council co-chair, MP Marc Garneau, protesting that foreign policy should not be dictated by ethnicity: A parliamentarian's ethnic origin gave no weight to a position. If the Liberal Party embraced this way of thinking — the way the Conservatives had done to bolster electoral support — there would be no way to manage foreign policy risks.

When Dion was at Foreign Affairs, Freeland served as minister of international trade. She was one of the Canadians barred from Russia once Moscow slapped Canada with retaliatory sanctions after Canada imposed sanctions on Russia for attacking Ukraine. Freeland put considerable energy into deepening relations with Ukraine and blocking all of Dion's initiatives to improve relations with Russia.

For example, on July 19, 2016, Dion went to the Prime Minister's Office to discuss relations with Russia. Several other ministers attended the meeting, including Freeland. Dion argued for the importance of dialogue with Moscow, especially since several Quebec companies were unable to access the Russian market because of sanctions, while other countries such as France were quite willing to sign contracts with the Russians. Dion also sought the prime minister's support for his upcoming meeting a week later with his Russian counterpart, Sergei Lavrov.

I learned that this discussion didn't go well. Freeland opposed any warming of relations with Russia. Trudeau vacillated, seemingly incapable of expressing any ideas about Canadian–Russian relations, and finally sided with Freeland.

Dion prepared his meeting with Lavrov. The civil servants sent his office an outline of the conversation he was to have with his Russian counterpart. The first item on the agenda was Ukraine. I nearly fell off my chair — I reminded Dion he was the minister of foreign affairs of Canada, not of Ukraine. The Ukrainian question should come up last. And I invited him to open the conversation in French, a language Lavrov speaks very well.

Right after the meeting between Dion and Lavrov, pro-Ukrainian pressure groups and even some members of the Ukrainian government blasted this timid rapprochement with Russia. In a weekly newspaper, closely followed by the Ottawa political elite, a representative of Canadians of Ukrainian origin denounced the meeting with Lavrov, demanding that Dion fall back into line and support the Ukrainian cause unconditionally.[21]

A few weeks later, in October 2016, the Ukrainian deputy foreign minister visiting Ottawa told *The Globe and Mail* his country was "not happy to see the Trudeau government resume co-operation with Russia over the Arctic."[22] Frankly, this was too much. I sent an email to Dion's chief of staff and all his political advisers, reminding them we were funding Ukraine's government, training their military and supporting their cause, and they should at least show us gratitude in return. I was told the Ukrainian official was being given a reality check from the deputy minister of foreign affairs in a meeting.

After Dion was fired in January 2017, relations with Russia quickly deteriorated. On becoming foreign affairs minister, Freeland took great delight in casting Russia as the greatest threat on the international scene. On June 6, 2017, in a speech outlining Canadian foreign policy in the House of Commons, Freeland made an outrageous comparison, equating Russia with the terrorists of the Islamic State[23] — at a time when the American and French presidents were meeting with President Vladimir Putin.

A few months later, the government drove the point home, adopting the *Justice for Victims of Corrupt Foreign Officials Act* and imposing sanctions on individuals "who are, in the opinion of the Government of Canada, responsible for, or complicit in, gross violations of internationally recognized human rights or acts of significant corruption."[24] Despite the universal scope of this act, it mainly targeted Russia. On November 3, 2017, Canada announced sanctions against around thirty Russians.

This attitude of extreme hostility surprised several foreign affairs experts. According to Irvin Studin, editor of the foreign policy magazine *Global Brief*, "a Canadian position that professes to support Ukraine or advance Canadian interests in Ukraine through outright, frontal hostility with Russia is, on this logic, an exercise in strategic idiocy: It helps neither Ukraine (which cannot thrive without Russian re-engagement) nor core Canadian interests in the Arctic (and Europe, for that matter) . . . Moreover, taken to its logical conclusion, this position could portend one of war with Russia — again, contrary to any Canadian interests in Ukraine, the Arctic and Europe — or indeed some manifestation of Russian destabilization, if not collapse."[25]

***

The Canadian government's eagerness to yield to the demands of pro-Ukrainian groups reveals its relative weakness as well as its fear of losing the electoral support of Ukrainian Canadians. On a more political level, it illustrates the power and influence different groups wield in promoting a cause, such as Ukraine, Israel or the Tamils of Sri Lanka. These groups regularly intervene in Canadian political life, particularly during election campaigns, when they can mobilize their supporters in key ridings, playing one party off the other.

Several observers have noted the increasing clout of these groups, especially during the Conservative years from 2006 to 2015. Stephen Harper's unconditional support for Israel and Ukraine was part of a well-oiled electoral strategy. In an interview in 2010, Immigration minister Jason Kenney described his role in cultivating ethnic support for the Conservative Party.[26]

Some people point out that this approach is dangerous, because it amounts to "unduly ethnicizing politics in Canada . . . It's a debasement, in a way, of our shared citizenship to appeal to particular groups so narrowly, in such a shallow way, just on the basis of identity."[27] Trudeau, then sitting on the Opposition benches, noted that "in the short term, [Kenney] has been effective at buying off certain groups . . ." But the Liberal Party "can actually propose a larger, more responsible view of where the country should be going, rather than just simply trying to buy off votes one group at a time."[28] Seven years later, the Trudeau government's positions on the Israeli-Palestinian conflict and the

Ukrainian question clearly showed the Liberal Party was acting in exactly the same way as the Conservatives.

Besides, Trudeau did everything he could to charm Canada's most active ethnic groups. A look at the Prime Minister's Office website in 2017 showed how thoroughly he treated his relations with certain countries and certain communities, saluting the national holidays of Armenia, South Korea, India, Israel, Pakistan, the Philippines and Poland. But the website didn't salute Mexico, Haiti, Lebanon, Greece or Italy, whose communities in Canada were large but no doubt less active politically. Trudeau also posted messages for the holy days of different faith communities, most notably the Sikhs and Tamils.

Many Canadian diplomats are frustrated by the growing influence on Canadian foreign policy of ethnic groups and interest groups. They are concerned this influence subordinates foreign policy to domestic policy and warps the defining and defending of Canada's national interests.

Christopher Westdal is a Canadian expert on Ukraine and Russia (he served as ambassador to Ukraine from 1996 to 1998, then to Russia from 2003 to 2006). He is sharply critical about the role of diasporas. "With all due respect for Ukraine, but also India, Sri Lanka and others, we fall into line with diasporas, which are often more motivated by anger and past conflicts than by Canada's national interests," he wrote in an email to me.[29]

Of course, diasporas are political stakeholders in this country just like other Canadians, and they can express their view of government policies affecting their countries of origin, he added. But that's not the point. According to Westdal, parties naturally seek ethnic votes, but once in power, "their leaders and ministers of Foreign Affairs need to rise above ethnic concerns and embrace a larger context to define and serve national interests." Which is not what's happening.

Ukraine is the most mediatized example of the ethnicization

of Canadian foreign policy, but it isn't the only one. According to Canada's former ambassador to the People's Republic of China, David Mulroney, one of the main impediments "to advancing our international interests more effectively is the steady encroachment of domestic policy considerations into our foreign policy calculations."[30] He particularly deplored the readiness of Canadian politicians to play the ethnic card towards Asian countries by always ensuring that delegations include Canadians of Chinese or Indian origin.[31]

During official trips, Canadian delegations shouldn't be "so relentlessly tailored to the ethnicity of the country being visited," he wrote. Such displays do not impress countries like China and India, according to Mulroney. "As proud as we are of our diversity," he added, "we need to remember that leaders in powerful and important countries such as India and China are focused on serious international issues," not on the ethnic composition of Canadian delegations.

Mulroney's criticism turned out to be premonitory. In February 2018, Trudeau made an official visit to India, accompanied by his family and four of his Cabinet ministers who are Sikhs. The Trudeau family decided to dress in Indian costume to please their official hosts. But things didn't turn out as expected. The Indian prime minister met with Justin Trudeau only at the very end of the visit. Indian, Canadian and world media had a field day ridiculing the prime minister for wearing "fancy dress." More seriously, a scandal erupted when it turned out an Indo-Canadian of the Sikh faith, convicted of the attempted murder of an Indian minister visiting Canada, was actually invited to a reception in New Delhi attended by Trudeau. Several observers blamed the incident on the Liberal Party's cozy relations with the Sikh community in Canada and particularly with its radical independence faction. In any event, this official visit turned out to be a complete failure, demonstrating what happens when politicians blindly solicit the support of cultural communities.

CHAPTER TEN
FLIRTING WITH CHINA

Justin Trudeau sometimes puts his foot in it. In November 2013, a few months after becoming leader of the Liberal Party of Canada, he made a slip of the tongue about China. He was asked during a public meeting which government he admired most. "There's a level of admiration I actually have for China," he replied. "Their basic dictatorship is actually allowing them to turn their economy around on a dime and say we need to go green, we need to start, you know, investing in solar."[1] His words came as a shock. Politicians ridiculed the young Liberal leader for his lack of judgment. Some analysts went further, suggesting he resembled his father, Pierre, who loved being provocative and was often suspected of sympathizing with dictatorships. Lysiane Gagnon, the celebrated columnist at *La Presse*, wrote that Justin Trudeau was no doubt trying to be provocative, "but he is not intellectually equipped for this kind of bravado."[2]

Justin's mistake nonetheless illustrates the Trudeau clan's fascination with China. Pierre Trudeau went to China twice before entering political life —travelling there the second time with Jacques Hébert, with whom he wrote *Two Innocents in Red China*, a remarkable book about the experience. In 1973, Pierre Trudeau went to Beijing as prime minister, then made a private trip to Tibet in 1979 after being defeated in the general election that year. With his sons Justin and Alexandre, he returned to China in 1990, shortly after the Tiananmen Square massacre. Alexandre maintained this family passion for China, visiting the country several more times and writing a long introduction and afterword to a new edition of *Two Innocents in Red China* in 2007. As a nod to his father, Alexandre brought out a new book in 2016, *Barbarian Lost: Travels in New China*, revealing his talents as an observer, analyst and essayist.

Pierre Trudeau and Jacques Hébert's approach to China was both original and controversial. They ventured along, wandering without any established plan, visiting cities, villages, monasteries, companies, hospitals, schools, restaurants. They met leaders, scholars, professors, workers. They discussed, argued, listened, laughed. The book was in the form of a road trip taken by two innocents. But innocent of what? "Innocent of not knowing any better," Pierre answered his son Alexandre.[3] Was that really the case? Alexandre wasn't convinced. "In truth, their innocence and implied lack of agenda were not entirely sincere," he writes. "They were really more like a rhetorical stance, a plea of innocence addressed to the court of public opinion."[4] In fact, Trudeau and Hébert had at least two objectives in publishing this work. They wanted to present the Canadian public with an image of Red China that contradicted Western anti-communist propaganda. Trudeau made no bones about this. In the introduction to the English edition of the book in 1968, he wrote: "There is at least one comment in the book which I believe to be as true today as it was when we left for Peking: '. . . it seemed to us imperative that the citizens of our democracy should know more about China.'"[5] The two authors also wanted to shake up Quebec society at a time when it was just emerging from the "Grande Noirceur" or Great Darkness of the Duplessis years, a period characterized by fierce anti-communism and the Catholic Church's stranglehold on society. But the book could be interpreted in an altogether different light. It could be seen as tacit support for an authoritarian regime. Trudeau's controversial visit to Cuba in 1976 confirmed this suspicion.

With *Barbarian Lost: Travels in New China*, Alexandre followed in his father's footsteps, describing how China had been transformed by reform and the effects of capitalism. He also recounts his own first experience of the country in 1990, along with his father and Justin, when the two brothers had fun climbing mountains and visiting temples and bazaars.[6]

Strangely enough, Justin Trudeau doesn't say a word about his family's fascination for China in his memoirs, *Common Ground*. He goes on at length about his job as a ski instructor in British Columbia, then about the bar scene with his buddies in Montreal. But he doesn't devote a single line to his father's book on China or to the long visit the family made to Beijing, although there is a family photo of him with his brother in Tiananmen Square.

Justin Trudeau's silence is all the more surprising considering that when he became prime minister on November 4, 2015, China had a central place in Canada's economic development and in international relations.

***

Pierre Trudeau's recognition of Red China in 1970 was visionary. At the time, the United States led an international boycott of communist China. Most states recognized Taiwan, where the Chinese nationalist government had settled following its defeat by the communists in 1949. The small island served as a major American base.

Trudeau found this situation absurd. He didn't agree with isolating a country with a billion citizens even if it had an abhorrent government. He started talks to establish relations with

Beijing under the auspices of mainland China's embassy in Sweden. The talks ran into the problem of Taiwan. For mainland China, Taiwan was Chinese territory and Beijing was the only legitimate government. Trudeau understood, but he refused to let drop Taiwan completely. After long discussions with External Affairs, he came up with a diplomatic formula that Beijing found persuasive: Recognizing a government doesn't necessarily equate recognizing all its territorial claims. Trudeau used a compelling analogy to get the message across: "I think that if a country wishes to recognize Canada we would not demand that it recognize, for example, our sovereignty in the Arctic."[7]

In a joint press release announcing the establishment of diplomatic relations between the two countries, Canada "took note" of the Chinese government statement on the inalienable character of its territorial integrity. China gained diplomatic recognition, and Canada didn't abandon Taiwan, although it had to break off official relations with the island. A dozen Western countries followed Trudeau's lead in recognizing mainland China, and Canada's actions opened the way to China replacing Taiwan at the UN General Assembly and on the UN Security Council in the fall of 1971.

Canada's new relations with China didn't provide concrete results at first. An initial trade mission in 1971 won a contract for Canadian wheat exports. It was only at the beginning of the 1980s that two-way economic relations really took off. Then relations cooled suddenly in 1989, after the Chinese government forcibly suppressed the Tiananmen pro-democracy movement. But Canada couldn't afford to hold back from China, especially since other Western countries moved quickly to normalize relations with Beijing. Canada was the last Western country to do so.[8]

In 1993, the new government led by Jean Chrétien made China a priority.[9] Chrétien's first international visit was to the APEC Summit in Seattle, where he met many Asian leaders, including the president of China. A year later, he led Team Canada, a big trade mission to Asia that headed to China first. About 500 Canadians joined Chrétien on the mission, including all provincial and territorial premiers, business people, journalists, academics and NGO leaders.[10] He headed a second trade mission to China several years later.

These missions "were innovative and effective in their day," writes Canada's former ambassador to China, David Mulroney.[11] In fact, they produced economic and political benefits. Trade with China rapidly increased. More importantly, Canadian investments in China also surged. Relations between the two countries strengthened to the point that by 2005, Chinese President Hu Jintao and Prime Minister Paul Martin spoke at an Ottawa meeting of a "strategic partnership."[12] This meant civil servants in Canada and China could work on a shared agenda, including delicate issues such as security, intelligence, counter-terrorism and many other subjects outside of the purview of strictly economic relations. At the same time, Martin was involved in setting up the G20, a forum designed to enable non-members of the G7, such as China, to take part more effectively in global governance. The G20 meetings of finance ministers started in 1999, and the G20 meetings of heads of state in 2008.

With the defeat of the Liberals in 2006, the Conservative Party assumed power and quickly took a split line on China. Some MPs and even some ministers showed open hostility towards improved relations with China, which they accused of religious persecution, human rights violations and industrial espionage.

Conservative leader Stephen Harper blew both hot and cold. Relations between Canada and the United States cooled in September 2005, when Washington refused to respect a trade ruling favouring Canada. Harper, then Opposition leader, retorted that Canada could withdraw from NAFTA and seek greater trade diversification, notably with China. If the US wouldn't play by the rules, then "we will have to put much higher emphasis on exploiting the growing demand of China, India and others for our natural resource sectors," he told his MPs.[13]

A year later, on becoming prime minister, Harper's enthusiasm for China waned. En route to the APEC Summit in Vietnam, he said he had no intention of changing the Canadian position on human rights in China just to favour trade with that country. Canadians "don't want us to sell that out to the almighty dollar," he said.[14]

From this point on, relations took on an ideological character and began deteriorating. The Harper government granted honorary citizenship to the Dalai Lama, receiving him officially. At every opportunity, the government denounced human rights violations in China and took pleasure in humiliating the Chinese ambassador in Ottawa. Harper even refused to attend the opening of the Beijing Olympic Games in 2008, unlike a hundred other heads of state and government who turned up there, including the American president, George W. Bush. The Harper government's ideological rigidity had a negative impact on relations with China, just as it was poisoning relations with other countries such as Russia. In his book, David Mulroney relates how, as Stephen Harper's diplomatic adviser from 2006 till 2009, he continually fought the prime minister's political adviser, warding off his extreme ideological impulses, which harmed Canadian diplomacy.[15]

China was not impressed by the Conservative government's behaviour, and actually ignored it. At the beginning of the 2000s, China was rapidly developing economically and was emerging as the world's second economic power. The country was imposing its power, whether economic, military, cultural or scientific, everywhere in the world. China now coveted Canada. "The first decade of the twenty-first century represented something of a Chinese rediscovery of Canada as an investment opportunity, an education provider, a vacation destination and a place to shop for property as a hedge against possible unwelcome developments at home," writes Mulroney.[16]

Paradoxically, political relations between the two countries were at a low point, but economic relations were rapidly developing, which undoubtedly explains why Harper changed course four years after becoming prime minister. Time was running out if Canada wanted to take advantage of China's extraordinary development. Canada was lagging behind by the time Harper charted this new direction. Paul Martin's much-vaunted "strategic partnership" with China had fallen by the wayside, and no annual meetings were held to discuss human rights. The Canadian and Chinese prime ministers avoided one another.

Canada's allies, meanwhile, headed for China. Australia understood that the tectonic plates of geopolitics and the economy had moved, and the time had come to adjust to the new reality. In 2007, Kevin Rudd became prime minister. He spoke fluent Mandarin and announced that Australian foreign policy was repositioning towards Asia while maintaining a strategic alliance with the United States. Chinese investment flooded into Australia. China's strong economic performance in the wake of the 2008 financial crisis further encouraged Westerners to turn to Beijing.

Harper took note of these changes. He broke the ice. In 2009, he refused to receive the Dalai Lama and headed for China on an official visit. He returned there in 2012 and 2014. Each visit marked an improvement in relations, extending the scope of cooperation to include an agreement on nuclear technology; an agreement on the promotion and protection of investment; the strengthening of scientific and cultural relations. Much remained to be done, in particular a free trade agreement China had been seeking for some time. Australia seized the day, announcing a strategic partnership with China in 2013, including an annual meeting of leaders accompanied by Cabinet consultations on political and economic questions.[17] A year later, the two countries signed a free trade agreement, after six years of negotiations.

***

As was mentioned earlier, China fascinated the Trudeau clan, and that included Justin. While serving as an MP he kept a low profile on the issue, but things changed once he entered the Liberal leadership race in 2012–2013. He got the chance to express his view on trade relations between the two countries when a Chinese state-owned company bought the Canadian oil and gas company Nexen. The transaction between Nexen and the China National Offshore Oil Corporation (CNOOC) led to vigorous debate about the foreign takeover of Canadian firms in strategic sectors. Some people, including in the Conservative government, were disturbed by the prospect of Chinese firms serving political objectives. This was not a new problem. Pierre Trudeau had instituted strict controls on foreign direct investment to prevent American companies from exerting undue influence on the Canadian economy. Harper amended the *Investment Canada Act*, allowing the government to review an investment if it could be injurious to "national security."

Trudeau supported the transaction. In an op-ed piece in the *Edmonton Journal*, he said the CNOOC-Nexen deal was good for Canada because it would offer economic benefits to the middle class.[18] The question of national security struck him as secondary. Canada faced a double reality in this case. Its domestic market was small and it could no longer count on the American market to stimulate growth. Canada needed to turn towards Asia, particularly China, which urgently needed raw materials and energy to drive its growth. Canada had to seize this opportunity. "By 2030, two-thirds of the planet's middle class will be in Asia," Trudeau wrote. "How we define and manage our relationship with Asian economies to play a Canadian role in fuelling that growth will matter as much to the Canadian middle class in this century as our relationship with the US did in the last."

Trudeau was aware that China's emergence as a great power had geopolitical and security implications for Canada and the rest of the world, but he wasn't worried about that. "China has a game plan," he wrote. "There is nothing inherently sinister about that." In the CNOOC-Nexen case, "Chinese ownership of three per cent of oilsands leases hardly constitutes a national security issue." In one fell swoop, Trudeau lifted Harper's idea from the 2006 elections, swearing to transform Canada into an "energy superpower," poised to benefit from the tremendous economic development of emerging countries such as China, Indonesia and India. A few days after Trudeau's op-ed appeared, the Conservative government approved the deal.

***

Paul Evans, a Canadian expert on Asia-Pacific questions, uses a striking phrase in describing how important China is for Canada. "For Canadians, China is no longer 'over there'; it is right here on our doorsteps," he writes.[19] At the same time, China still inspires fear among many Canadians because of its closed and authoritarian political system, its stance on human rights and its rapid emergence as a global power. "What should be our strategic response to global China?" Evans asks. "Should China be approached as a friend, strategic partner, ally, competitor, adversary or enemy?"[20]

Trudeau didn't see things the same way. His op-ed in the Edmonton Journal set no pre-conditions and pursued no geopolitical or ideological ulterior motives. The op-ed showed that for Trudeau, Canadian–Chinese relations come down, ultimately, to dollars and cents. Trudeau maintained this line. The February 3, 2015, session of the International Affairs Council was partly devoted to Canada's trade relations with China and India. Trudeau was then in the Opposition. He said nothing about human rights or the rise of China as a great power or its sometimes brutal attitude towards its neighbours over its territorial claims in the South China Sea. Trudeau and the Council members made some recommendations to develop economic relations with China and promote a better understanding of China in particular and Asia in general. They suggested that a future Liberal government revive the strategic partnership (with frequent meetings between the Canadian and Chinese prime ministers), consider the consequences for Canada of China's rise, promote investment in Canada by the Chinese diaspora and revive Team Canada missions, with the difference that this time Chinese investors and donors would be invited to Canada.

The Council members also noted the lack of knowledge and ambivalence of many Canadians about the prospect of Canada increasingly turning towards the Pacific: It was proposed to increase knowledge about Asia among students, companies and the employees of federal, provincial and municipal governments in Canada.

The Liberal platform during the 2015 election said nothing about China and Asia, but once in power the new Liberal government made a priority of redefining Canadian–Chinese relations. At the G20 summit in Turkey in November 2015, the Chinese president Xi Jinping showered Canada with praise, while reminding Justin Trudeau of his father's extraordinary vision in establishing relations with the People's Republic of China forty-five years earlier.[21] Throughout the winter and spring of 2016, the Prime Minister's Office and several ministries, mainly Foreign Affairs and International Trade, but also Health, Finance and Heritage, worked on a new strategy to strengthen relations between the two countries. Some of the International Affairs Council's suggestions from a year earlier found their way into the new strategy. This was the first time since 1987 that Canada sought to reformulate relations with China and on such a large scale: In fact, all government ministries were consulted.[22] The Cabinet adopted the new strategy in May 2016.

The strategy had four structural elements: restoring the central character of Canada's relations with China; undertaking annual dialogue between prime ministers; initiating discussions on a free trade agreement; and promoting interpersonal links, notably in the domains of education and tourism. The strategy called for the creation of permanent dialogue structures to institutionalize relations.

The Foreign Ministers' Dialogue was thus set up to discuss current and future bilateral questions relating to foreign policy, such as human rights, regional and international security, the environment and climate change, the rule of law and legal co-operation. The High-Level National Security and Rule of Law Dialogue was also set up. The two sides set short-term objectives for co-operation around two major themes: initiating discussions on an extradition treaty and a treaty on the transfer of convicted offenders, as well as related questions; and pursuing discussions on cooperation in the areas of cybersecurity and fighting cybercrime.

A dialogue structure involving the Royal Canadian Mounted Police and Chinese law enforcement was also set up to facilitate cooperation on justice and the suppression of crime. Two other forums were established: one devoted to finance and the economy, and the other to health. Finally, Canada announced that 2018 was to be the year of Canada–China tourism.

This strategy was applied during Trudeau's visit to China at the end of August 2016 and the visit of his Chinese counterpart to Canada a month later. On these occasions, the two prime ministers signed dozens of trade agreements, revived the strategic partnership and began preliminary discussions on a free trade agreement. The most remarkable thing about Trudeau's strategy of reviving relations between the two countries was the skill with which he and his government raised the issue of human rights. They addressed the issue in the context of the rule of law — a constructive approach, since the Chinese government was prepared to discuss the rule of law, but preferred keeping civil rights off the table.

The question of human rights had been a major Canadian concern during the first years of the Harper government. It was still mentioned at every meeting and in every speech, but always obliquely. For example, when Prime Minister Trudeau addressed business people in Shanghai, he buried the subject of human rights in the middle of a long speech saluting China's progress "on governance and the rule of law."[23]

The prime minister and his government steered away from controversy on another topic: the growing tension between China and several neighbouring states over territorial and economics claims in the South China Sea. For several years, China had sought to project its sovereignty onto this maritime area by taking possession of some disputed islands: 30 per cent of world trade transited these waters. The controversy had military implications, since control of the passage was at stake, but also economic implications, because of offshore oil exploitation here, as well as an abundance of fish. Most countries of the region were opposed to Chinese claims and received support from the United States. There were occasional incidents involving naval and commercial ships. Here again, Canada kept a low profile. It opposed unilateral measures while being careful not to name China directly.

The government's position was nonetheless clear. Ottawa called on all parties to work towards a solution in full respect of international law, without resorting to military action, which would likely harm regional security and stability.

Trudeau returned to China a second time at the beginning of December 2017. The visit failed to achieve its objectives: The two countries agreed to put off free trade negotiations until a later date. This is where the matter could have rested, except that an unexpected event came out of the blue to shake up relations between the two countries. On December 1, 2018, Meng Wenzhou, the chief financial officer of the telecommunications giant Huawei, was catching a connecting flight at the Vancouver airport when Canadian police officers swept in to arrest her, acting at the request of American authorities who wanted her extradited. She was accused of circumventing the American embargo against Iran.

Suddenly, Canada was stuck in the middle of the trade dispute that had flared up between the United States and China since Donald Trump's election. Canada was wedged between the world's two leading economic powers, which were also important trading partners. Ottawa tried to calm the situation, claiming that justice would be served. Unfortunately, the Canadian government hadn't expected China to react so harshly to the arrest. Within days, Chinese police arrested former diplomat Michael Kovrig and businessman Michael Spavor. They were accused of endangering China's security. The whole incident sent shock waves through the Canadian political class. Ottawa called unsuccessfully for the immediate release of the two men, and China demanded that the Chinese national be released. Each side made aggressive statements that did nothing to calm things down. With all the noise this situation generated, and the gaffes made by Canadian diplomats, Canada's ambassador to China, John McCallum, resigned on January 27 at the request of the prime minister for having suggested Meng Wenzhou had strong legal grounds for avoiding extradition to the United States. At the time of writing, the crisis between the two countries had still not been solved.

***

To return to that striking phrase of Paul Evans — "Should China be approached as a friend, strategic partner, ally, competitor, adversary or enemy?" — China is too complex a country to be reduced to a simple formula. China is at one and the same time a friend to Canada, but not in the same way as the United States or France; a strategic partner, but only in certain areas, whether economic, diplomatic or legal; an ally in the fight against climate change; a competitor in some areas of trade; and an adversary in the great game that is emerging for influence in the South China Sea. It remains to be seen if China is actually an enemy.

Will the sharp tensions stirred up by the Huawei affair transform Canada's relations with China? Possibly. But it's important to keep a sense of perspective. Relations with a great power should be measured over the long term. Trudeau has chosen his camp. He has publicly stated that China is a strategic partner. This is only normal. The profound geopolitical upheavals in the world that are redistributing power are naturally driving Canada towards China. The planet is no longer dominated by the United States; new powers, mainly in Asia, are emerging and taking up significant geopolitical and economic positions on the world scene. China in particular is no longer solely a manufacturing economy, but is becoming one of the world's leading scientific and technological innovators.

Since Pierre Trudeau's day, Canada has been seeking to diversify its trade relations to loosen the American grip on the Canadian economy. The new world in the making provides Canada with just such an opportunity. If Justin Trudeau's rapprochement with China produces the results hoped for when the strategy was adopted in May 2016, this will be his greatest foreign policy success.

CHAPTER ELEVEN
DONALD TRUMP'S DISRUPTIVE PRESIDENCY

Canada's relationship with the United States is one of the most intense relationships between any two countries in the world. For better or for worse, the two countries are deeply intertwined in economic, political, social, military and cultural terms. Tearing this relationship apart could cause serious damage.

The relationship is so strong that an incoming Canadian prime minister generally goes to the United States for his first official visit abroad. Justin Trudeau was no exception: He and his wife headed to Washington in March 2016. But this visit was out of the ordinary. It was the first protocol visit for a Canadian prime minister in nineteen years, and was capped by a state dinner attended by the who's who of American political, economic and cultural life.

President Barack Obama hosted the event with great style, marking his political and ideological proximity to Trudeau. "Your election and the first few months in office have brought a new energy and dynamism not only to Canada but to the relationship between our nations," Obama said, clearly relieved he was no longer hosting Stephen Harper, with whom relations had deteriorated over the Conservative government's last months in office.

During the evening, the most glamorous political couples of the world lined up for selfies and photos. But as Obama and Trudeau were celebrating the Canadian–American alliance, Democrats and Republicans everywhere across the United States were getting ready for the next presidential election that November.

Hillary Clinton won the Democratic nomination. The Republicans, meanwhile, were in the throes of an extraordinary nomination race. Billionaire Donald Trump led an unconventional campaign, breaking with the Republican party establishment, breaking all the rules of decency by abundantly insulting his opponents, both Republican and Democratic, and calling into question every dogma of economic and social liberalism adopted by elites since the postwar years. The strategy worked. Trump won several primaries, to the astonishment of even the most informed observers. He forced one fellow candidate after another to withdraw. The political and media class in Ottawa was amused to follow Trump's no-holds-barred race for the Republican nomination, as if this were playing out like *Game of Thrones*, but for real. Surely decency would prevail, people said in the corridors of power. Surely the Republican Party would pull itself together and choose a more presentable candidate.

But then Donald Trump won the nomination. He was now energized ten-fold. His angry base of voters claimed Washington elites were abandoning entire American communities — white men, people living in deindustrialized regions and the smaller agricultural states, excluded from the new economy — and acting to benefit other American communities such as racial and sexual minorities, liberal elites, Silicon Valley and the larger states.

As soon as Trump won the nomination, he took on a more radical tone, driving home a populist and xenophobic message. "America First" wasn't just a slogan — it was an entire program of withdrawal, protectionism and the rejection of liberal values. He proposed wedging a wall between Mexico and the United States to keep out what he called "drug dealers and rapists"; he drew up a list of Muslim countries whose citizens he wanted to bar from

entering the United States; he called into question US membership in NATO and other military alliances; he questioned the
terms of all free trade agreements, including the one with Canada
and Mexico; he accused China of "raping" Americans with its
"unfair" trade practices; he said most African countries should be
recolonized for a century because they understood nothing about
leadership. As for Hillary Clinton, the Democratic nominee, he
called her "crooked Hillary" to her face, even during TV debates.

In Ottawa, some of us in Minister Dion's office were starting to
get worried about the US presidential campaign, although it was
too soon to panic. Opinion polls showed Clinton with a comfortable lead, and we in Ottawa had to believe American common sense
would ultimately prevail. But then on the evening of November
8, Trump won the presidency, thanks to one of the quirks of the
American electoral system, where it is not the popular vote that
dictates who wins, but the majority of electoral votes in the College
of Electors. Trump won the majority of the College of Electors,
although he got 46 per cent of the popular vote, compared to
Clinton's 48 per cent. The difference was made by just 70,000 votes
in three states that had previously voted for Obama.

***

Once Trump took office, the question remained whether he was
still willing to upset the liberal international order and replace it
with a transactional system based on bilateral relations that the
United States would always be able to dominate. This question
was vital for Canada, whose foreign policy and economic prosperity were based on the international order in place since the end of
the Second World War.

The key features of the liberal order were multilateralism,
the key role reserved for international organizations in regulat-
ing relations between countries, the respect for rules established

by treaties, the promotion of democracy and freedom, collective security, and free trade between nations. These features structured the liberal order — not only ensuring its survival for more than seventy years, but also, since the fall of the Berlin Wall in 1989, allowing it to welcome into its midst former "enemies," particularly those in the Eastern bloc. Even communist China adopted some of the features of the liberal order by increasingly participating in the system of collective security through the UN Security Council and accepting international trade rules through its membership in the World Trade Organization.

As I noted in earlier chapters, Canada is one of the beneficiaries of this liberal order. Canada owes its prosperity and security not just to its proximity to the United States, but also to its active participation in the international system established since 1945. And, according to former Prime Minister Joe Clark, Canada is able to use the balance between the US and the international system, wielding greater clout on the world scene than the size of our population and economy alone would normally allow. As Clark notes in his most recent book, maintaining strong relations with the United States and playing an independent role in the world are two sides of the same coin.

> *"Our access to Washington has added real clout to the standing we have earned independently by our actions in other countries. When Canada's relations with Washington are strong, other countries come to us, or listen to us, not just because of our own merits, but because we could influence the superpower. By the same token, our positive reputation in the world . . . has been an asset the United States has not always been able to command itself."[1]*

Canada benefits from its privileged relationship with the United States and its place in the world. Several analysts believe the Canada–US Auto Pact of 1965 — a pact that was highly advantageous to Canada — stemmed from Lester B. Pearson's decision a year earlier to send Canadian peacekeepers to Cyprus, preventing war there between two American allies, Greece and Turkey. Twenty-five years later, during the Gulf War, Brian Mulroney, an ardent defender of multilateralism, convinced George H. W. Bush to work through the UN in setting up a multinational coalition to oust Iraq from Kuwait.

The economy is at the heart of this relationship. The North American Free Trade Agreement (NAFTA), signed initially by Canada and the United States, and then by Mexico in the late 1980s, turned North America into the world's leading trade bloc. NAFTA enabled Canada to increase trade with its partners to the south and is a model for Canada's economic and commercial strategy abroad. Accordingly, under the Harper government, Canada signed several bilateral free trade agreements — with Colombia, Israel and South Korea — as well as multilateral agreements with the European Union and with Asia–Pacific countries (the Trans-Pacific Partnership). The Trudeau government sought to strengthen Canada's trade arrangements by undertaking negotiations with China and India, two countries that many experts believe will be the world's two leading economies by 2030.

The Canadian–American relationship also has its drawbacks. Today, about 75 per cent of Canada's trade is with the United States. This trade structure has not changed since 1970, when Pierre Trudeau recommended diversifying Canada's trade around the world, expanding well beyond its bilateral relationship with the United States. There can be no doubt about it: Canada's prosperity greatly depends on its privileged relationship with the United States, but Canada's very dependence on its superpower neighbour has an impact on Ottawa's foreign policy choices.

At the end of the Second World War, Canada became the third power of the Free World after the United States and the

United Kingdom. This status enabled Canada to be a key partici-
pant in establishment of the liberal order. Other countries sought
Canada out and respected its voice. But those days are long past.
France, Germany and Japan quickly returned to the international
scene. The creation of the European Union relegated Canada to
middle-power status, in relative isolation on the North American
continent. It was only with great difficulty that Canada succeeded
in getting into the G7, at Washington's express request. Canada
had some room to manoeuvre in its relations with the US (refusing
to take part in the Vietnam War, then in the 2003 invasion of Iraq),
but "Canada must, in all its calculations, take American interests
into account," according to several experts. "Ignoring this dimen-
sion would have far graver consequences for Canada than for most
other States" maintaining relations with the United States.[2]

Donald Trump's election makes this analysis even more relevant.
The new president's erratic, unpredictable and nationalist character forced the Canadian government to be vigilant at all times, no
matter what political positions it takes. America swung in a new
direction and Ottawa had to take this change into account.

***

Even before Donald Trump shook up the political, economic
and military order of the world, Trudeau anticipated several
profound changes that were likely to transform the international
system in general and American society in particular and force
Canada to review its traditional practices. In fact, protectionism had been part of American political discourse for several
years. Obama negotiated the Trans-Pacific Partnership, but
Democratic candidate Hillary Clinton opposed it. Clinton's
rival, Senator Bernie Sanders, ran on a left-wing program
including elements of anti-globalization and nationalism resem-
bling some of Trump's positions. Economic and geopolitical

power was moving from the Western world towards the Asia-Pacific region, which explains why President Obama decided to reorganize American military operations abroad, refocusing them on the Asia-Pacific region.

In an article Trudeau wrote about China's acquisition of the Canadian oil and gas company Nexen, he supported the transaction because of Asia's vital importance for the Canadian economy. "For much of our history, the only trading relationship that mattered was with the United States," he wrote. "That was the 20th century. The 21st century is different . . . We can no longer rely on the United States alone to drive our growth."[3] Trudeau aimed high. Asian countries, he wrote, were investing trillions of dollars in infrastructure. That growth required exactly the kind of expertise Canada has. "What if our goal was to become Asia's designers and builders of livable cities? What if we got our world-class financial institutions and pension funds together with our world-class engineering and construction industries to secure a leadership role for Canada in Asia's growth?"

Access to Asian markets was undoubtedly coveted by all Western countries, but for Canada the reality remains that its number one relationship is with the United States. Trudeau knew this perfectly well. As Liberal Party leader, then as prime minister, he gave two lyrical speeches on Canadian–American relations. "We're actually closer than friends," he told president Obama during the state dinner at the White House. "We're more like siblings."[4] He acknowledged that Canada needed to diversify and globalize its approach to trade and foreign investment, but he added that Canadians "must see our own future in the future of North America."[5] Donald Trump's decision to completely renegotiate or even abolish NAFTA came as a stark reminder for Canada's political and economic class. A grim reality stared Canada in the face: It was the next-door neighbour of the world's leading power and was isolated from the rest of the planet.

***

In Ottawa, Trudeau consulted his most important ministers —
Foreign Affairs, International Trade, Public Safety, National Defence,
Finance — on how to respond to Trump's astonishing election. The
policy directors of all the ministers got together to anticipate how the
new US administration would act. They held simulations, imagin-
ing a situation and then speculating about the president's possible
answers based on his previous statements as a candidate.

It became increasingly clear that the new American government
was so unpredictable, Canada could not reliably foresee its actions.
But the Trudeau government still needed a strategy to better
understand its relationship with the new administration taking
over the White House on January 20, 2017. Towards the end of
December, this strategy began to take shape. The former prime
minister and father of NAFTA, Brian Mulroney, said on every
public occasion he could just how well he thought of Trump, whom
he had known for twenty years. He quickly positioned himself as
an intermediary between Ottawa and Washington, and it worked.
Trudeau discreetly contacted Mulroney, asking him to use his
contacts to moderate the fervour of the new president. At the same
time, the prime minister sent his principal secretary, Gerald Butts,
and chief of staff, Katie Telford, to Washington, to meet as many
of Trump's advisers as possible and to plead Canada's case.

The Prime Minister's Office, the Privy Council, the Canadian
embassy in Washington as well as the ministries of Foreign Affairs
and International Trade prepared an offensive in American
political, economic and cultural circles to underline the importance of relations between the two countries. The Ministry of
International Trade published a twelve-page document providing
Canadian diplomats, MPs, senators, ministers and their advisers
with common talking points in interactions with their American

counterparts. The document outlined trade and employment statistics as well as information on border security and energy. This strategy targeted the president's behaviour directly, influencing his inner circle and Congress. But Ottawa also targeted the thirty-five American states whose economies depended considerably on trade with Canada. State governors, legislators, local chambers of commerce, mayors of large cities and local media were also solicited by their Canadian counterparts. The Trudeau government left nothing to chance. American decision makers at every level of responsibility were contacted. The stakes were huge. Ottawa had to avoid an economic and political disaster between the two countries.

Trudeau believed that a new strategy required new team players. This explains his decision, on January 6, 2017, to fire Stéphane Dion, replacing him with Chrystia Freeland, then minister of international trade. The prime minister was convinced Dion didn't have the profile needed for interactions with the new administration. Another aspect of Ottawa's strategy towards the United States was to avoid antagonizing the president and his advisers. Trudeau had concerns about Dion's at times caustic manner and academic approach. But there was actually another lesser-known reason for Dion's dismissal, which I noted in chapter five: Relations between Trudeau and Dion were terrible, and Trudeau saw Trump's election as the perfect opportunity to get rid of his minister.

Freeland seemed by all appearances to be the right person at the right time. In international trade, she had shown diplomatic skill in finalizing the free trade agreement with the European Union. She spoke English, French, Russian and Ukrainian fluently. A career journalist, she had been posted in Kiev, Moscow, London and New York, mostly for leading media outlets such as the *Financial Times*, *The Economist*, *The Globe and Mail* and Reuters news agency.

In 2013, Freeland won a Toronto by-election for the Liberals. She was a good catch for Trudeau, who had just been elected party leader. She strengthened the Liberal Party's economic team in the House of Commons.

It was said Freeland had an impressive list of contacts in the United States. But did she have the right contacts? After all, she represented the left wing of the Liberal Party, and her articles appeared in liberal media that were openly hostile to Trump. Besides, Freeland had written a devastating book about the super-rich, like the men in the new president's inner circle. In *Plutocrats: The Rise of the New Global Super Rich and the Fall of Everyone Else*, she attacked elites cut off from the rest of society whose ever-growing wealth threatened the social fabric.

Trudeau presented Freeland as the person for the job. She was the new minister of foreign affairs, and unlike her American and Mexican counterparts, she would be directly involved in NAFTA negotiations. In Washington, neither Secretary of State Rex Tillerson nor Commerce Secretary Wilbur Ross would take part in talks. A special envoy was assigned to the task. The Mexicans counted on their secretary of the economy.

Freeland was a formidable negotiator. Supported by the experienced chief negotiator Steve Verheul and a team of some forty Canadian diplomats, she led talks with the Americans and Mexicans with an iron hand for more than a year, even remaining in Washington a few days at a time when the going got tough. President Trump repeatedly threatened to break off the talks, withdraw from NAFTA and negotiate bilateral agreements with his two partners. In June 2018, at the G7 summit in Charlevoix, frictions between Canada and the United States over tariffs on Canadian steel and aluminum led to such animosity between Trump and Trudeau that observers feared a trade war was on the point of breaking out, which would have a devastating impact on the Canadian economy.

But it was not to be. On September 30, 2018, after weeks of intense negotiations, the three countries announced just one hour before the midnight deadline fixed by Trump that they had concluded the Canada–United States–Mexico Agreement (CUSMA) for a sixteen-year term. Once ratified, CUSMA would replace NAFTA. The new agreement wasn't perfect, and Canada had to make concessions in several areas, such as the important dairy, poultry and eggs industry. Also, some observers noted Article 32.10, requiring CUSMA countries to inform the other two signatories three months in advance if they planned to begin free trade negotiations with non-market economies. If an agreement was signed with a non-market economy, Article 32.10 allowed the other signatories to terminate CUSMA and replace it with a bilateral agreement. Article 32.10 was widely considered to be specifically aimed at China and would hinder Canada's ability to negotiate a free trade agreement with that country.[6]

***

The trend towards North American integration wasn't just apparent in economic and commercial terms. Security was also a key feature of Canadian–American relations — border security between the two countries, continental security against external threats and global security. Security considerations may even be said to lie at the heart of the relationship between Canada and the United States. Shortly before the Second World War, the Americans realized that if Canada, a large, sparsely populated and weakly defended country, were to fall into enemy hands, this would constitute a "threat" to US security. On a visit to Kingston in 1938, president Franklin Delano Roosevelt declared: "I give to you assurance that the people of the United States will not stand idly by if domination of Canadian soil is threatened by any other empire."[7] Prime Minister Mackenzie King got the message loud and clear. Canada would prevent attack "either by land, sea or air to the United States across Canadian territory."[8]

At the time, what experts call the "Kingston Dispensation" marked the genesis of the Canadian–American military alliance.

This seems the most natural of alliances, and is determined by geography, political and cultural ties, a common language and shared values. The two countries are closely interwoven in a unique fabric of agreements, treaties, accords and official military links. Military relations extend well beyond the official framework, since they cover civil industry, universities and private institutions.

Over the years, Canada and the United States have woven closer military ties through discussion and collaboration. The Canadian Ministry of Defence and the Pentagon increased the number of agreements to include the exchange of weather data and the deployment of nuclear weapons. Canadian officers often completed their studies at major American universities and military training centres. Over time, they joined military units as part of officer exchange programs.

Ottawa and Washington signed an agreement on sharing development and production of military equipment, integrating their respective defence industries even more closely. Several other agreements enabled the United States to test new weapons on Canadian territory. Finally, creation in 1957 of the North American Aerospace Defence Command (NORAD), countering the Soviet nuclear air threat (ballistic missiles and bombers), marked the crowning achievement of Canadian–American military integration. From then on, the North American continent was "considered to constitute a single territory and the air forces of the two countries were placed under unified command."[9] The NORAD commander is always an American general and the deputy commander a Canadian general.

Security relations took a new turn following the terror attacks of September 11, 2001. The Americans demanded that security measures for the North American continent be completely overhauled. In particular, they considered security at the Canadian border to be lax, and wanted it tightened. None of the nineteen Middle Eastern terrorists implicated in 9/11 had crossed the Canada–US border to commit the attacks, but two years earlier, a terrorist of Algerian origin who was living in Montreal had taken a ferry from British Columbia to Washington State with the intention of bombing the Los Angeles airport. He was exposed at the border and arrested by US customs officials just as he was about to flee. The threat of terrorism incited the two countries to negotiate several agreements reinforcing controls at the border, in airports and at ports.

As some experts have noted, the Kingston Dispensation has had consequences for Canada.[10] If Canada is unable to do its share in defending the continent, the United States will assume this responsibility. This has had repercussions globally. Once the Al Qaeda leadership moved to Afghanistan after 9/11, the United States targeted them. Canada quickly joined the multinational intervention in Afghanistan, as much out of interest as conviction.

***

Canada's security relationship with the United States was practically trouble-free for about fifteen years. But Trump's election risked subjecting Canada to strong turbulence. The president didn't question North American military integration, because this served the fundamental interests of the United States. That wasn't the problem. Actually, Trump's vision of the world conflicted with Canada's. He disrupted the foundation of the liberal international order to which Canadians adhered. He attacked NATO, undermined international organizations by withdrawing from UNESCO and reducing American funding of the UN, withdrew from the Paris Agreement on Climate Change and systematically refused to criticize Russia, which had violated the principles of international law by annexing Crimea.

The American president's challenges to the international order posed a dilemma for Canada. Either it lined up with American positions, thus losing any independence, or it took a combative stance and risked clashing with its one and only true partner on the international scene.

Canada had to face the reality that its dependence on the United States was bound to increase as long as political, economic and military elites in Ottawa and elsewhere in the country saw Canada's relationship with the United States as the only way to guarantee benefits and safeguard national security. Experts on Canadian foreign policy are definite on this point: Since the Kingston Dispensation, "Canadians not only had to articulate their security policy in terms of threats (if any) facing the country, but also in terms of threats facing the United States. In short . . . Canadians now had to accept Washington's definition of threats and security strategies, even if Canadians didn't agree."[11] Once Trump became president, this observation became even more worrisome than before.

Was there any way for Canada to loosen America's grip without having to choose between the United States and the rest of the world?

Chrystia Freeland thought she had found the solution. She gave a speech in the House of Commons on June 6, 2017.[12] Ostensibly, this was a statement about foreign policy, but it came almost two years after the Liberal Party had gained power, and while it purported to cover Canada's relations with countries around the world, it focused mostly on the United States. Freeland tried hard to avoid criticizing the Americans too much. Before giving the speech, she even phoned her American counterpart, Rex Tillerson, to discuss it, something that was not publicly known.

This speech came a week after Washington's decision to withdraw from the Paris Agreement on Climate Change. The move sent shock waves around the world, to the point that Emmanuel Macron, the president of France (the agreement's host country), addressed the American people directly in English to criticize the decision.

Freeland noted this decision, which followed a series of events that were shaking up the world order. "International relationships that had seemed immutable for 70 years are being called into question," she said. "From Europe to Asia, to our own North American home, long-standing pacts that have formed the bedrock of our security and prosperity for generations are being tested," she added, alluding to Russia's annexation of Crimea, Islamist terror and China's bold claims in the South China Sea. These events required Canada to "think carefully and deeply about what is happening and find a way forward."

The minister was particularly concerned about what was happening south of the border. "On behalf of all Canadians," she thanked the enormous contribution of the United States to the postwar order. "In blood, in treasure, in strategic vision, in leadership, America has paid the lion's share" to ensure stability, she said, which had benefited Canada for seven decades. But recently, many American voters "cast their ballots animated, in part, by a desire to shrug off the burden of world leadership." We respect this choice, she said. But Canada was being forced to adapt. "The fact that our friend and ally has come to question the very worth of its mantle of global leadership puts into sharper focus the need for the rest of us to set our own clear and sovereign course. For Canada, that course must be the renewal, indeed the strengthening, of the post-war multilateral order."

Freeland made a highly accurate assessment of Canada's situation compared to the United States, but all she could offer by way of a solution was for Canada to promote its own sovereignty. Nowhere in her speech did she outline a strategy of action. Instead, she listed a series of principles, without mentioning concrete measures to implement them.

Words and pictures can't replace ideas and actions. Freeland knows Canada is a "prisoner" of its relationship with the United States. Appealing to the gallery won't change this grim reality.

AFTERWORD

After the October 2015 election, Justin Trudeau had the flexibility to implement a detailed and original foreign policy agenda. This agenda would have revived the great Canadian tradition of diplomatic activism from before the Conservative victory in 2006 while taking account of new geopolitical realities. But what has he done? As the end of Trudeau's mandate as prime minister approaches, the question is worth asking, especially since his former diplomatic adviser, Roland Paris, has come out with sharp criticism of Trudeau's foreign policy.

In his blog at the University of Ottawa, Paris wondered when and how the prime minister would "convert his global celebrity into action."[1] Trudeau now has the opportunity to have a lasting impact on international politics, writes Paris, "on specific issues, and to use his high global standing to rally international action." Paris is fully aware of how fluid politics can be. The opportunity shouldn't be missed. "Whatever cause Trudeau may choose, it would be a shame if he did not make full use of his 'global political capital' while it lasts . . . Other Canadian PMs have accomplished great things with much less international visibility."

Indeed, all Canadian prime ministers over the last fifty years have had an impact on Canadian foreign policy by taking controversial or bold decisions, often from the very first years of their mandate.

Pierre Trudeau recognized communist China, developed closer relations with Southern countries and started a campaign to reduce nuclear weapons. Brian Mulroney negotiated the free trade agreement with the United States, led the worldwide campaign against apartheid in South Africa and created La Francophonie along with French president François Mitterrand. Jean Chrétien adopted a new philosophy — human security — that ultimately led to the Ottawa Convention on the Prohibition of Anti-Personnel Mines and the creation of the International Criminal Court. Chrétien decided against Canada's involvement in the war in Iraq. Stephen Harper developed the maternal, newborn and child health initiative for developing countries and pursued negotiations on free trade agreements with Europe and Asia-Pacific countries, as well as the Paris Agreement on Climate Change.

Trudeau has so far undertaken no major international initiative. Now that he has laid aside many of the proposals contained in the Liberal Party program, how does he plan to develop the vision — the big picture — that will enable his government to have an impact on the world scene? Stéphane Dion had energy and ideas, but he didn't have the prime minister's confidence. Chrystia Freeland was named to replace Dion supposedly to remedy this deficit. And yet the foreign policy speech she gave on June 6, 2017, left a lot to be desired.

Freeland started her speech with a question: "Is Canada an essential country, at this time in the life of our planet?"[2] In response, she then listed a series of contributions by Canada and Canadians to building the international order in which we live and that ensure our prosperity and security. "Canada believes strongly that this stable, predictable international order has been deeply in our national interest." The international order has undoubtedly been good for Canada, but it only seems to be stable. The principles, institutions and procedures of the international order are increasingly being challenged.[3]

Growing competition and power relations between states are creating upheaval on the global scene and undermining international institutions. Power is being fragmented, and we are seeing the emergence of a new world grouped around regional centres of influence, each dominated by a single great power. International law is being trampled underfoot (the United States in Iraq, Russia in Ukraine, China in the South China Sea) by the very powers that are supposed to be upholding it. Emerging powers such as China, Brazil and India are asserting their ambitions and trying to reinvent the global rules for geopolitics, finance and trade that were set in place by the victors just after the Second World War. Other states, such as Russia, but also several members of the European Union and of NATO, such as Turkey, Poland and Hungary, are challenging the liberal character of this order while promoting authoritarian rule. Even the United States is affected by this upheaval. Donald Trump is a compelling symptom of it. And yet the only answer Freeland gave in her speech is that Canada will fight hard to maintain and strengthen the existing world order. This is what Canada's essential role on the world scene amounts to.

Defending an international order that has been so good for Canada is a noble cause. But defending this order shouldn't seem like some rearguard action, and Freeland's speech has every appearance of being just that. She doesn't try to explain the challenges to the world order. Canada would make an original contribution to building a new world order by acknowledging the deep-seated causes of the crisis challenging the world instead of clinging to the old order.

Trudeau and Freeland don't see the world the way it is shaping up to be: They see it the way it should be. This attitude might have made sense in the aftermath of the Second World War, when everything had to be rebuilt from scratch. But this is no longer the case today. With each passing day, Canada is losing influence in the world. Canada's G7 membership, for example, conceals the fact that Canada is no longer among the world's seven leading economic powers, but the tenth. Sometime in 2019, South Korea is expected to knock Canada into eleventh place.

As we said earlier in the chapter on the United States, President Donald Trump has shaken up the world order without distinguishing between friends and enemies. He has rocked the foundations of the world order that were patiently built up since 1945 and seems to be offering nothing to replace it. His actions follow a pattern. In 2003, the United States violated all international standards by invading Iraq, causing the deaths of 200,000 people and creating a political and humanitarian disaster that extended well beyond Iraqi borders. With his America First approach to foreign policy, Trump's unilateralism consists in promoting American interests to the detriment of the country's allies. It remains to be seen if this approach will be pursued after the Trump years or whether Americans will eventually return to multilateralism. I am not optimistic on this score.

We were expecting a lot from China, but the arrest of one of the top executives at Huawei is there to remind us that great powers have no friends, they only have interests. Canada is not as blameless in this affair as it may at first appear: Things could have been handled with more finesse and in a way less prejudicial to Canada itself. Ottawa justified arresting the Huawei executive at the Americans' request by invoking the rule of law, but should have used better political judgment. Canada now finds itself in the uncomfortable position not of being essential for the resolution of this political and trade conflict between Washington and Beijing, but of being stuck between two superpowers on whom our prosperity depends. The outcome of this affair will necessarily disappoint one or the other of the great powers without offering any benefit to Canada.

The Liberal government has also succeeded muddying the waters with Russia and India. Canada had every reason to impose sanctions on Moscow for its actions in Ukraine, but there was no reason to freeze all relations with Russia. It is too often forgotten that Canada has just two neighbours — the United States and Russia — both of whom are great powers at present. We need a smart and productive relationship with Moscow. Instead, Freeland has resorted to robust Cold War rhetoric at a time when most Western countries are trying to re-engage with Russia. Trudeau's disastrous trip to India in March 2018 set relations back with that country, but a more serious problem is the murky relationship the Liberals maintain with the radical fringes of the Sikh independence movement resident in Canada. For this reason, New Delhi is not putting much stock in its relations with Canada.

But it's not only the great powers that are shaking up Canada. Saudi Arabia is a true terrorist state: We have only to consider the Saudi kidnapping of the Lebanese prime minister, the war of extermination in Yemen, the covert links with terrorist groups in the Middle East, the latent conflict with Qatar, the financing of extremist Koranic schools around the world. In summer 2018, when the Canadian Foreign Affairs minister sought the release of three Saudi activists who were arrested for demanding their basic rights, the Saudi government swiftly moved to break with Canada. But Ottawa didn't slap sanctions on the Saudi regime, doubtless because it feared losing the $15-billion contract to build armoured vehicles in Ontario.

Canada's relations with all these powers have deteriorated, for a multitude of reasons. The Liberal government now finds itself in an exceptional situation: Its relations are tense, not to mention poor, with four of the world's great powers: the United States, Russia, China and India. Moreover, it has lost influence over Arab and Muslim countries by adhering to a staunchly pro-Israel policy, has an ongoing conflict with Saudi Arabia and is neglecting Africa. Things do not augur well for the next vote for a non-permanent seat on the UN Security Council in June 2020. Canada will be competing with Norway and Ireland for one of the two seats reserved for Western countries.

***

Freeland's speech on the essential character of Canada in the twenty-first century seems like a rhetorical exercise in an age when international relations are characterized by brutality. To suggest, as Freeland does, that "We are now called — by virtue of our unique experience, expertise, geography, diversity and values — to do this again, for a new century" seems like magical thinking when we consider how the Canadian government has reduced foreign assistance, cut back on our involvement in UN peacekeeping, rejected dialogue with countries whose politics we dislike and blocked the development of the diplomatic corps by freezing its budget. To be effective, any foreign policy needs powerful means that can be mobilized quickly in service of a well-crafted and forward-looking strategy. Without these means and without this strategy, Canada will come across only as a glib but powerless country. Canada needs to do better if we are to face up to the turbulence of the new world order now dawning.

ACKNOWLEDGEMENTS

This book is dedicated to my long-time friend Elaine Potvin, who has also been my hard-working colleague for some twenty years. I owe her a lot. I wish to thank her for rereading the French version of this work and proposing many changes that enhance the text while making it more accessible to non-specialists.

Thanks also to the team at Québec-Amérique for their work on the original French edition. Martine Podesto in particular believed in this work from our very first meeting. Thanks to Éric St-Pierre for his work in editing and revising the text and for helpful comments and criticism that enabled me to achieve greater focus.

While writing this book, I also benefited from the knowledge and views of many people, some of whom prefer to remain anonymous. Thanks especially to the political scientists Yvan Cliche and Jean-François Caron, who reread part of the text, and to former ambassador Christopher Westdal for his guidance on Ukraine and Russia.

I also wish to thank James Lorimer & Company, who believed in this book and mobilized a team of professionals so it could reach an English-language readership as quickly as possible. A special word of thanks to the translator, George Tombs.

Finally, I wish to thank Justin Trudeau and Stéphane Dion, who allowed me to join their team of advisers and gave me the opportunity to take part in defining some features of the Liberal government's foreign policy. Of course, in thanking them, I do not in any way imply they are responsible for the opinions expressed in this work, or the facts contained herein.

ENDNOTES

Foreword

1. Bruce Cheadle, "Trudeau says image-making part of governing, not a popularity contest," The Canadian Press, December 17, 2015.

Chapter One

1. Jacques Hébert and Pierre Elliott Trudeau, *Two Innocents in Red China*, 1968, and Douglas & McIntyre, 2007.
2. Pierre Trudeau, "Pearson ou l'abdication de l'esprit," *Cité libre*, April 1963.
3. Jack L. Granatstein and Robert Bothwell, *Pirouette: Pierre Trudeau and Canadian Foreign Policy*, University of Toronto Press, 35.
4. Kim Richard Nossal, Stéphane Roussel and Stéphane Paquin, *Politique internationale et défense au Canada et au Québec*, Les Presses de l'Université de Montréal, 2007, 77.
5. Granatstein and Bothwell, *Pirouette*, 34.
6. Nossal, Roussel and Paquin, *Politique internationale et défense au Canada et au Québec*, 298.
7. Granatstein and Bothwell, *Pirouette*, xiii.
8. Trudeau, *Common Ground*, HarperCollins, 2014, 86.
9. Ibid., 79.
10. Ibid.
11. Ibid., 81.
12. Ibid., 102–103.
13. Ibid., 103.
14. Ibid., 19.
15. Jean Chrétien, *My Years as Prime Minister*, Vintage Canada, 2008, 291.
16. Trudeau, *Common Ground*, 104–106.
17. Ibid., 107.
18. Ibid.
19. Ibid.
20. Diana Juricevic, "Playing the Rights Card," *Literary Review of Canada*, December 2012, 5.
21. Trudeau, *Common Ground*, 166.
22. The author of this book won the Liberal nomination in the Outremont riding.
23. Trudeau, *Common Ground*, 106–107. In the author's opinion, the verb "visit" is inappropriate here: Trudeau made most of these trips with his father at a young age and in an official setting that limited what they could experience. It would be more accurate to say Justin Trudeau "went to" a hundred countries but "visited" only twenty of them before being elected an MP.
24. Trudeau, Common Ground, 311.

Chapter Two

1. *Hansard,* June 11, 2009.
2. Trudeau, *Common Ground*, 331.
3. Justin Trudeau, "Why CNOOC-Nexen Deal is Good for Canada," *Edmonton Journal*, November 19, 2012.
4. Meetings took place on May 2, June 19, August 26, September 22 and December 3, 2014, and on February 3 and May 12, 2015.
5. No minutes were kept during the meetings of February 3 and May 12, 2015.
6. Speech given by Liberal leader Justin Trudeau at the Canada 2020 conference, October 2, 2014.
7. Ibid.
8. Mike Blanchfield, "You'll Face Consequences from Canada if You Take Israel to International Criminal Court: Baird to Palestinians," *National Post*, March 6, 2013.
9. Mike Blanchfield, *Swingback: Getting Along in the World with Harper and Trudeau*, McGill-Queen's University Press, 2017, 9.
10. Ibid., 33.
11. Ibid., 39.
12. Stephen Harper and Stockwell Day, "Canadians Stand with You," *The Wall Street Journal*, March 28, 2003.
13. Kenneth Whyte, "In Conversation: Stephen Harper," *Maclean's*, July 5, 2011.
14. Blog of July 14, 2011.
15. Roland Paris, "Baird's Silence on Abuses in Bahrain Exposes Canada's Inconsistency," *The Globe and Mail*, April 5, 2013.
16. Ibid.
17. Roland Paris, "Time to Make Ourselves Useful," *Literary Review of Canada*, March 2015, 13.
18. Lee Berthiaume, "A Return to Multilateralism: Meet Roland Paris, the Man Behind Justin Trudeau's Foreign Policy," *National Post*, December 29, 2015.

Chapter Three

1. *Real Change*, Liberal Party of Canada, 2015, 68–71.
2. Roland Paris, "Canada's Decade of Diplomatic Darkness," *The Globe and Mail*, September 24, 2014.
3. Roland Paris, "Are Canadians Still Liberal Internationalists? Foreign Policy and Public Opinion in the Harper Era," *International Journal*, vol. 69, no. 3, 2014, 274–307.
4. Blanchfield, *Swingback*, op. cit.
5. Ibid., 196.
6. "The Canadian Opportunity," speech given by the prime minister at the World Economic Forum, January 20, 2016.

Chapter Four

1. Chrétien, *My Years as Prime Minister*, 54.
2. Ibid., 154.
3. The other foreign policy advisers were Christopher Berzins, a civil servant at Foreign Affairs: besides being policy director, he covered the United States, Europe and security questions; Jean Boutet, a civil servant at Environment Canada and Dion's former adviser when he served as minister of the environment: Boutet took care of Latin America, the environment and the Arctic; Laurence Deschamps-Laporte, an academic: she dealt with the Middle East and some security issues; Pascale Massot, a professor at the University of Ottawa specializing in China: she mainly covered China and East Asia; Andrew Sniderman, a jurist interested in human rights, LGBTQ issues and some security issues. Dion was dismissed on January 6, 2017; the incoming minister, Chrystia Freeland, dismantled the team in February 2017, retaining only Laurence's services.
4. I served as adviser from February 22, 2016, to February 10, 2017.
5. Nossal, Roussel and Paquin, *Politique internationale et défense au Canada et au Québec*, 270.
6. Ivan Head and Pierre Trudeau, *The Canadian Way: Shaping Canada's Foreign Policy*, 1968–1984, McClelland and Stewart, 1995, 317.
7. Ibid.
8. Max Weber, *Politics as a Vocation*, ed. and trans. Tony Waters and Dagmar Waters (2015). Submitted to "Weber's Rationalism and Modern Society" (2015). This passage has been slightly modified by this translator.
9. "Building a Foreign Policy for Canada," speech by Stéphane Dion, Ottawa Forum 2016, January 28, 2016.
10. "A Guiding Principle for Canada in the World," speech by Stéphane Dion, March 29, 2016.
11. *Hansard*, vol. 148, no. 119, December 1, 2016.
12. Geoffrey A. H. Pearson, *Seize the Day: Lester B. Pearson and Crisis Diplomacy*, Carleton University Press, 1993, 79.
13. Nossal, Roussel and Paquin, *Politique internationale et défense au Canada et au Québec*, 331.
14. Ibid., 116.
15. Paris, "Are Canadians Still Liberal Internationalists?"
16. Speech given by Stéphane Dion at the second St. Laurent Forum on International Security, May 6, 2016.
17. Speech given by Stéphane Dion to the Montreal Council on Foreign Relations, October 17, 2016.
18. On this subject, see Jean-François Caron, *Affirmation identitaire du Canada, Politique étrangère et nationalisme*, Athéna éditions, 2014.

Chapter Five

1. Telephone interview with the author, January 17, 2018.

2. Marc Semo, "Laurent Fabius, pedagogue de la diplomatie hollandiste," *Le Monde*, November 17, 2016.
3. *Mandate letter of the Minister of Foreign Affairs*, Prime Minister's Office, November 2015.
4. Eddie Goldenberg, *The Way It Works: Inside Ottawa*, Doug Gibson Books, 2007, 232.
5. Ibid., 233.
6. Chrétien, *My Years as Prime Minister*, 156.
7. Eddie Goldenberg, *The Way It Works*, 234.
8. Chrétien, My Years as Prime Minister, 157; Goldenberg, *The Way It Works*, 235.
9. Justin Trudeau, *Common Ground*, 167.
10. Ibid., 170.
11. Ibid., 171.
12. Ibid., 172.
13. Ibid., 173.
14. Ibid., 173.
15. Eddie Goldenberg, *The Way It Works*, 233.
16. Ibid., 233.
17. Cabinet meetings are attended by all ministers, whereas committee meetings are attended only by those ministers directly concerned.
18. Steven Chase, "Dion Adviser Critical of Saudi Arms Deal," *The Globe and Mail*, March 28, 2016, 1.
19. Jocelyn Coulon, "Une autre guerre de Trente Ans ?" *La Presse*, January 10, 2016.
20. A few weeks later, Dion accepted the appointment as ambassador to Berlin and special envoy to the European Union.
21. Linda Diebel, *Stéphane Dion: Against the Current*, Viking Canada, 2007, 166.

Chapter Six

1. United Nations General Assembly A/67/PV.44, November 29, 2012, https://unispal.un.org/DPA/DPR/unispal.nsf/0/C05528251EA6B4BD852 57AE5005271B0.
2. Ibid.
3. Dennis Shanahan and Joe Kelly, "Fears Julia Gillard Isolated by Adviser on UN Palestinian Vote," *The Australian*, December 1, 2012.
4. Editorial: "Canada Should Not Penalize the Palestinians," *The Globe and Mail*, November 30, 2012.
5. The Security Council consists of five permanent members — China, the United States, France, the United Kingdom, and Russia — and ten non-permanent members chosen on a regional basis and elected by the General Assembly for a two-year mandate.
6. At that time the UN had 192 member states. In 2011, South Sudan

became the 193rd member.

7. Speech given by Prime Minister Stephen Harper at the UN General Assembly, September 23, 2010, www.un.org/ga/search/view_doc. asp?symbol=A/65/PV.11.

8. Helen Buzzetti, "Confusion autour de l'appui américain," *Le Devoir*, October 16, 2010, A3.

9. Ibid.

10. CTV News staff, "Did the US Snub Canada at the UN Vote?" October 14, 2010.

11. Germany's aggressive campaigning for a seat on the Security Council is worth noting. After joining the UN in 1973, Germany has sought a Council seat on five occasions, compared to Canada's six candidacies for a seat since 1945.

12. Paris, "Time to Make Ourselves Useful."

Chapter Seven

1. Canadian Press, "Trudeau Announces Bid for Seat on UN Security Council," *National Post*, March 16, 2016.

2. *Real Change*, Liberal Party of Canada, 64.

3. Andrew Cohen, *Lester B. Pearson*, Penguin Canada, 2008, 101.

4. Costanza Musu, "Canada and the MENA Region: The Foreign Policy of a Middle Power," *Canadian Foreign Policy Journal*, vol. 1, no. 18, 2012, 72.

5. Nossal, Roussel and Paquin, *Politique internationale et défense au Canada et au Québec*, 300.

6. Mulroney, Memoirs, 364.

7. Chrétien, *My Years as Prime Minister*, 347.

8. Steven Seligman, "Canada and the United States General Assembly (1994– 2015): Continuity and Change Under the Liberals and Conservatives," *Canadian Foreign Policy Journal*, 2016, vol. 22, no. 3, 276–315.

9. Ibid., 276.

10. Ibid., 277.

11. Ibid., 308.

12. Ibid., 310.

13. Paris, "Time to Make Ourselves Useful."

14. Jeffrey Simpson, "Truculent Moralizing for a Domestic Audience," *The Globe and Mail*, February 4, 2012.

15. Paul Lungen, "46 Per Cent of Canadians Negative Toward Israeli Gov't: Poll," *Canadian Jewish News*, February 22, 2017.

16. Graeme Hamilton, "Riding War Rages over Jewish State: Mount Royal," *Edmonton Journal*, October 2, 2015, and Patrick Martin, "Diverse Jewish Views Come to the Fore: Despite the Tories' Realignment of the Political Landscape in 2006, Liberals and NDP Are Back as Kosher Options for Many," *The Globe and Mail*, October 7, 2015, A14.

17. According to a report in *La Presse* on January 28, 2017, on companies and

organizations actively engaged in lobbying in Ottawa in 2016.

18. He did, however, restore funding for the United Nations Relief and Works Agency for Palestine Refugees, funding that the Conservatives had frozen.

19. Chrétien, *My Years as Prime Minister*, 356.

20. Liberal Party of Canada, "Letter to Michèle Asselin, Executive Director of AQOCVI," October 9, 2015.

21. Speech given by International Development minister Marie-Claude Bibeau unveiling Canada's first "feminist international assistance policy," June 9, 2017.

22. Head and Trudeau, *The Canadian Way*, 94.

23. CCCI, *Implementing Canadian Ambitions Supporting Global Development in Budget 2018*, 2.

24. Ibid.

25. Speech given by Prime Minister Justin Trudeau before Canada 2020, June 23, 2015.

26. On March 19, 2018, Ottawa announced it was sending a contingent of Blue Helmets to Mali.

Chapter Eight

1. Caron, *Affirmation identitaire du Canada*.

2. Francis Fukuyama, "Guidelines for Future Nation-Builders," in Francis Fukuyama, ed., *Nation-Building Beyond Afghanistan and Iraq*, The Johns Hopkins University Press, 2006, 233.

3. Ministry of National Defence, *White Paper of 1994*, 24.

4. James Appathurai and Ralph Lysyshyn, "Lessons Learned from the Zaire Mission," *Canadian Foreign Policy*, vol. 5, no. 2, Winter 1998, 100.

5. Jocelyn Coulon, *Les Casques bleus*, Éditions Fidès, 1994, 273.

6. For the events and reasons leading to Canadian involvement in Afghanistan, see Janice Gross Stein and Eugene Lang, *The Unexpected War: Canada in Kandahar*, Viking Canada, 2007.

7. David Morin, "Le côté obscur de la force: l'unité nationale, victime collatérale de la 'nation guerrière' de Stephen Harper," *Études internationales*, vol. 44, no. 3, 2013, 447.

8. Paris, "Are Canadians Still Liberal Internationalists?"

9. Ibid., 305.

10. *Real Change*, Liberal Party of Canada, 68.

11. Speech given by Prime Minister Trudeau at the Vancouver Conference, November 15, 2017, 3.

Chapter Nine

1. Blanchfield, *Swingback*, 169ff.

2. www.nato.int/cps/us/natohq/declassified_137930.html

3. Mulroney, *Memoirs*, 883.

4. Chrétien, *My Years as Prime Minister*, 361–62.

5. Speech given by Vladimir Putin at the Munich Conference, Novosti Press Agency, February 10, 2017.

6. Dominique de Villepin, *Mémoire de paix pour temps de guerre*, Éditions Grasset, 2016, 246.

7. Speech given by Minister Dion to the 62nd General Assembly of the Atlantic Treaty Association, October 11, 2016.

8. Chrétien, *My Years as Prime Minister*, 357.

9. The G7 is not an international organization but rather an informal forum for discussion. A G7 member acts as host for each meeting, and various participants are consulted on which additional countries may be invited.

10. External Affairs, *Foreign Policy for Canadians*, 1970, 68.

11. National Defence, *Challenge and Commitment*, 1987, 11.

12. Ibid., 51–52.

13. By the Antarctic Treaty of 1959, the twelve signatories set aside Antarctica as a neutral continent for scientific purposes. The treaty freezes territorial claims, protects the environment and bans military activity there.

14. Andrea Charron, Joël Plouffe and Stéphane Roussel, "The Russian Arctic Hegemon: Foreign Policy Implications for Canada," *Canadian Foreign Policy Journal*, vol. 18, no. 1, 2012, 38–50.

15. Joseph Trevithick, "Russia Projects Heavy Airpower in the Arctic from Constellation of New and Improved Bases," *The Drive*, January 2, 2019.

16. "Building a Foreign Policy for Canada's Future," speech given by Minister Dion, Ottawa Forum 2016, January 28, 2016.

17. "A Guiding Principle for Canada in the World: Responsible Conviction," speech given by Minister Dion at the University of Ottawa, March 29, 2016.

18. Ibid.

19. Michael Byers, "Towards a Canada–Russia Axis in the Arctic," *Global Brief*, Winter 2012, 22.

20. Speech given by Parliamentary Secretary Goldsmith-Jones, on behalf of Minister Dion, marking the twentieth anniversary of the Arctic Council, September 29, 2016.

21. Oksana Bashuk Hepburn, "Canada Should Do More for Ukraine," *The Hill Times*, August 10, 2016, 10.

22. Steven Chase, "Arctic Conference Draws Concern from Ukraine," *The Globe and Mail*, October 3, 2016.

23. Speech given by Minister Freeland, June 6, 2017.

24. Global Affairs Canada, "Canada Imposes Sanctions on Individuals Linked to Human Rights Violations and Corruption," press release, November 3, 2017.

25. Irvin Studin, "Canada's Four-Point Game: Part II," *Global Brief*, Winter 2018, 14.

26. Joe Friesen, "The 'Smiling Buddha' and His Multicultural Charms," *The Globe and Mail*, January 29, 2010.

27. Ibid.
28. Ibid.
29. Email exchange with the author, October 16, 2017.
30. David Mulroney, *Middle Power, Middle Kingdom: What Canadians Need to Know about China in the 21st Century*, Allen Lane, 2015, 14.
31. Ibid., 15.

Chapter Ten

1. Jen Gerson, "At Toronto Fundraiser, Trudeau Seemingly Admires China's 'Basic Dictatorship,'" *National Post*, November 8, 2013.
2. Lysiane Gagnon, "Le Jeune et la Chine," *La Presse*, November 14, 2013.
3. Hébert and Trudeau, *Two Innocents in Red China*, 3.
4. Ibid., 2–3.
5. Hébert and Trudeau, *Two Innocents in Red China*, 36.
6. Alexandre Trudeau, *Barbarian Lost: Travels in New China*, HarperCollins, 2016, 7.
7. Head and Trudeau, *The Canadian Way*, 224–25.
8. Mulroney, *Middle Power, Middle Kingdom*, 261.
9. Jean Chrétien, *My Years as Prime Minister*, 371.
10. Ibid., 294.
11. Mulroney, *Middle Power, Middle Kingdom*, 54.
12. Ibid., 262.
13. "Harper Roars but Lacks Bite on Trade," *Toronto Star*, September 9, 2005.
14. CBC website, "Won't 'Sell out' on Rights Despite China Trade: PM," November 15, 2006.
15. Mulroney, *Middle Power, Middle Kingdom*, 19.
16. Ibid., 23.
17. Ibid., 271.
18. Justin Trudeau, "Why CNOOC-Nexen Deal is Good for Canada."
19. Paul Evans, "Dancing with the Dragon," *Literary Review of Canada*, April 2013, 3.
20. Ibid.
21. See Minister Dion's speech marking the forty-fifth anniversary of diplomatic relations between Canada and China, January 27, 2016, 2.
22. Huhua Cao and Vivienne Poy, *The China Challenge: Sino-Canadian Relations in the 21st Century*, University of Ottawa Press, 2011, 51–56.
23. Speech given by the prime minister before the Canada–China Trade Council during his visit to China, September 1, 2016.

Chapter Eleven

1. Joe Clark, *How We Lead: Canada in a Century of Change*, Random House Canada, 2013, 135.
2. Nossal, Roussel and Paquin, *Politique internationale et défense au Canada et au Québec*, 79.

3. Justin Trudeau, "Why CNOOC-Nexen Deal is Good for Canada."
4. Speech given by the prime minister during the state dinner, March 10, 2016.
5. Speech given by Justin Trudeau at Canada 2020, June 23, 2015.
6. Wenran Jiang, "Under USMCA, Canada is Neither Strong nor Free," *The Globe and Mail*, October 10, 2018.
7. www.queensu.ca/encyclopedia/r/roosevelt-franklin-delano
8. policyoptions.irpp.org/magazines/defending-north-america/defending-the-united-states-and-canada-in-north-america-and-abroad.
9. Nossal, Roussel and Paquin, *Politique internationale et défense au Canada et au Québec*, 64.
10. Ibid., 62.
11. Ibid.
12. *Hansard*, speech by the minister of foreign affairs, June 6, 2017.

Afterword

1. Roland Paris, "When and How Will Trudeau Convert His Global Celebrity into Action?" blog, University of Ottawa, August 5, 2017.
2. Speech given by Minister Freeland, June 6, 2017.
3. Serge Sur, "Une société internationale en quête de repères," *Questions internationales*, no. 85–86, May–August 2017, 4–11.

SELECTED BIBLIOGRAPHY

James Appathurai and Ralph Lysyshyn, "Lessons Learned from the Zaire Mission," *Canadian Foreign Policy*, vol. 5, no. 2, Winter 1998.

Lee Berthiaume, "A Return to Multilateralism: Meet Roland Paris, the Man Behind Justin Trudeau's Foreign Policy," *National Post*, December 29, 2015.

Mike Blanchfield, "You'll Face Consequences from Canada if You Take Israel to International Criminal Court: Baird to Palestinians," *National Post*, March 6, 2013.

Mike Blanchfield, *Swingback: Getting Along in the World with Harper and Trudeau*, McGill-Queen's University Press, 2017.

Hélène Buzzetti, "Confusion autour de l'appui américain," *Le Devoir*, October 16, 2010.

Michael Byers, "Toward a Canada-Russia Axis in the Arctic," *Global Brief*, Winter 2012.

Canadian Council for International Cooperation, *Réalisation des ambitions du Canada: soutien au développement international dans le budget 2018*, October 2017.

Canadian Press, "Trudeau Announces Bid for Seat on UN Security Council," *National Post*, March 16, 2016.

Huhua Cao and Vivienne Poy, *The China Challenge: Sino-Canadian Relations in the 21st Century*, University of Ottawa Press, 2011.

Jean-François Caron, *Affirmation identitaire du Canada. Politique étrangère et nationalisme*, Athéna éditions, 2014.

CBC website, "Won't 'Sell out' on Rights Despite China Snub: PM," November 15, 2006.

Andrea Charron, Joël Plouffe and Stéphane Roussel, "The Russian Arctic Hegemon: Foreign Policy Implications for Canada," *Canadian Foreign Policy Journal*, vol. 18, no. 1, 2012.

Steven Chase, "Dion Adviser Critical of Saudi Arms Deals," *The Globe and Mail*, March 28, 2016.

Steven Chase, "Arctic Conference Draws Concern from Ukraine," *The Globe and Mail*, October 4, 2016.

Bruce Cheadle, "Trudeau Says Image-making Part of Governing, Not a Popularity Contest," *The Canadian Press*, December 17, 2015.

Jean Chrétien, *My Years as Prime Minister*, Ron Graham Books, 2007.

Joe Clark, *How We Lead: Canada in a Century of Change*, Random House Canada, 2013.

Andrew Cohen, *Lester B. Pearson*, Penguin Canada, 2008.

Jocelyn Coulon, *Soldiers of Diplomacy: The United Nations, Peacekeeping, and The New World Order*, University of Toronto Press, 1998.

Jocelyn Coulon, "Une autre guerre de Trente Ans ?" *La Presse*, January 10, 2016.

CTV News Staff, "Did the U.S. Snub Canada at the UN Vote?" October 14, 2010.

Department of External Affairs, *Foreign Policy for Canadians*, Government of Canada, 1970.

Department of National Defence, *Challenge and Commitment*, Government of Canada, 1987.

Department of National Defence, *White Paper of 1994*, Government of Canada, 1994.

Linda Diebel, *Stéphane Dion: Against the Current*, Viking Canada, 2007.

Paul Evans, "Dancing with the Dragon," *Literary Review of Canada*, April 2013.

Joe Friesen, "The 'Smiling Buddha' and his Multicultural Charms," *The Globe and Mail*, January 29, 2010.

Francis Fukuyama, "Guidelines for Future Nation-Builders," in *Nation-Building: Beyond Afghanistan and Iraq*, Francis Fukuyama (ed.), Johns Hopkins University Press, 2006.

Lysiane Gagnon, "Le Jeune et la Chine," *La Presse*, November 14, 2013.

The Globe and Mail Editorial Board, "Canada Should Not Penalize the Palestinians," *The Globe and Mail*, November 30, 2012.

Eddie Goldenberg, *The Way It Works: Inside Ottawa*, Doug Gibson Books, 2007.

Jack L. Granatstein and Robert Bothwell, *Pirouette: Pierre Trudeau and Canadian Foreign Policy*, University of Toronto Press, 1990.

Graeme Hamilton, "Riding War Rages over Jewish State: Mount Royal," *Edmonton Journal*, October 2, 2015.

Stephen Harper and Stockwell Day, "Canadians Stand with You," *The Wall Street Journal*, March 28, 2003.

"Harper Roars but Lacks Bite on Trade," *Toronto Star*, September 9, 2005.

Ivan Head and Pierre Trudeau, *The Canadian Way: Shaping Canada's Foreign Policy, 1968–1984*, McClelland & Stewart, 1995.

Jacques Hébert and Pierre Trudeau, *Two Innocents in Red China*, 1968 and Douglas & McIntyre, 2007.

Oksana Bashuk Hepburn, "Canada Should Do More for Ukraine," *The Hill Times*, August 10, 2016.

Wenran Jiang, "Under USMCA, Canada Is Neither Strong nor Free," *The Globe and Mail*, October 10, 2018.

Diana Juricevic, "Playing the Rights Card," *Literary Review of Canada*, December 2012.

Liberal Party of Canada, "Letter to Michèle Asselin, Executive Director of AQOCI," October 9, 2015.

Liberal Party of Canada, *Real Change*, 2015.

Paul Lungen, "46 per cent of Canadians Negative Toward Israeli Gov't: Poll," *Canadian Jewish News*, February 22, 2017.

Patrick Martin, "Diverse Jewish Views Come to the Fore: Despite the Tories' Realignment of the Political Landscape in 2006, Liberals and NDP are Back as Kosher Options for Many," *The Globe and Mail*, October 7, 2015.

David Morin, "Le côté obscur de la force: l'unité nationale, victime collatérale de la 'nation guerrière' de Stephen Harper?" *Études internationales*, vol. 44, no. 3, 2013.

Brian Mulroney, *Memoirs*, Random House, 2007.

David Mulroney, *Middle Power, Middle Kingdom: What Canadians Need to Know about China in the 21st Century*, Allen Lane, 2015.

Costanza Musu, "Canada and the MENA region: The Foreign Policy of a Middle Power," *Canadian Foreign Policy Journal*, vol. 1, no. 18, 2012.

Kim Richard Nossal, Stéphane Roussel and Stéphane Paquin, *Politique internationale et défense au Canada et au Québec*, Les Presses de l'Université de Montréal, 2007.

Roland Paris, "Baird's Silence on Abuses in Bahrain Exposes Canada's Inconsistency," *The Globe and Mail*, April 5, 2013.

Roland Paris, "Canada's Decade of Diplomatic Darkness," *The Globe and Mail*, September 24, 2014.

Roland Paris, "Are Canadians Still Liberal Internationalists? Foreign Policy and Public Opinion in the Harper era," *International Journal*, vol. 69, no. 3, 2014.

Roland Paris, "Time to Make Ourselves Useful," *Literary Review of Canada*, March 2015.

Roland Paris, "When and How Will Trudeau Convert His Global Celebrity into Action?" blog, University of Ottawa, August 5, 2017.

Geoffrey A. H. Pearson, *Seize the Day: Lester B. Pearson and Crisis Diplomacy*, Carleton University Press, 1993.

Steven Seligman, "Canada and the United Nations General Assembly (1994–2015): Continuity and Change under the Liberals and Conservatives," *Canadian Foreign Policy Journal*, vol. 22, no. 3, 2016.

Marc Semo, "Laurent Fabius, pédagogue de la diplomatie hollandiste," *Le Monde*, November 17, 2016.

Jeffrey Simpson, "Truculent Moralizing for a Domestic Audience," *The Globe and Mail*, February 4, 2012.

Janice Gross Stein and Eugene Lang, *The Unexpected War: Canada in Kandahar*, Viking Canada, 2007.

Irvin Studin, "Canada's Four-Point Game. Part II," *Global Brief*, Winter 2018.

Serge Sur, "Une société internationale en quête de repères," *Questions internationales*, nos. 85–86, mai–août 2017.

Joseph Trevithick, "Russia Projects Heavy Airpower in the Arctic from Constellation of New and Improved Bases," *The Drive*, January 2, 2019.

Alexandre Trudeau, *Barbarian Lost: Travels in the New China*, HarperCollins, 2016.

Justin Trudeau, "Why CNOOC-Nexen Deal is Good for Canada," *Edmonton Journal*, November 19, 2012.

Justin Trudeau, *Common Ground*, HarperCollins, 2014.

Pierre Elliott Trudeau, "Pearson ou l'abdication de l'esprit," *Cité libre*, April 1963.

Dominique de Villepin, *Mémoire de paix pour temps de guerre*, Éditions Grasset, 2016.

Max Weber, *Le savant et le politique*, Éditions 10/18, 2002.

Kenneth Whyte, "In Conversation: Stephen Harper," *Maclean's*, July 5, 2011.

Huguette Young, *Justin Trudeau: The Natural Heir*, Dundurn, 2015.

INDEX